Linux Revisited

Linux Revisited

S.B.Asoka Dissanayake

Asokaplus

Asokaplus

Contents

Chapter 01

Prologue

It was long time ago, that I started my blog site, the Linux-100.

Since then I have written few books on Linux.

I thought of updating those books for the current users.

Linux is 20 years young and my total immersion in Linux is only 15 years old.

Updating those books is an uphill task in the way the Linux has blossomed.

Besides, if I update my books, they lose their historical value.

This book is not about updating the old themes.

If I use the word update, it loses its scientific meaning, since from the time this book goes from preparation into its publication, the Linux would have changed its face, significantly.

The word revisiting may be more appropriate.

Linux fundamentals are moving forward very fast but their is an anticlimax with the emergence of smart phones and Android making inroads into the Linux World. Conventional Linux is fast losing its steam with new technology emerging and side stepping the desktop base seriously and smart phones making niche in the IT world, in particular.

Please do not forget Android is Linux based but proprietary driven operating system with lot of loopholes.

I am not going to discuss, kernel changes, configuration changes like init and systemmd and any implementation strategies of Linux in this book, which are actually the domain of the Linux developers.

The reader is advised to subscribe to Linux Magazine for cutting edge developments.

What I am trying here is to get an average Linux user who has migrated from Windows or Apple Mac to get his / her bearings right and the productive life jump started and feel free and liberated from hawk eyed proprietary propaganda.

Gnome 3 is out and I am beginning to love it even though, I come from the old and more organized KDE desktop base. But I have changed a lot now and I do not want a bulky desktop using all the resources at boot up, like Windows operating system does. With cloud computing taken its root, what one need is a simple desktop and a lightweight browser, which Peppermint uses in style.

I am an early adopter of Peppermint.

In Linux unlike, Windows one has many choices to adopt from the front end of your operating system derived from X-Windows system.

I am not going to delve into those fashionable themes too.

But the latest Debian DVD has solved that problem too, with six or more desktops to adopt in one installation which is already installed in my old IBM computer.

This was the way the old Suse (KDE based) worked but it did not have Gnome, then.

Then of course the latest Knoppix 7.5 is out which uses LXDE desktop and it has everything one needs and one need not buy a DVD or download it if you subscribe to Linux Magazine. I continue to download and test Linux distributions almost on weekly basis (used to be on daily basis in 2010) but the DVD that comes monthly with the Linux Magazine has made me to pace my steps leisurely.

But then again, there are over 300 live distributions out there.

I have to do justice to them.

Hence, this book comes out to make busy workers do not have to sweat a lot, looking for the latest Linux distribution and all enthusiastic Linux developers do not lose face that few customers are using their creations.

It is a question of choice.

The customer (average Linux user) is always right is my attitude.

What one needs is not luring but informed choice, freedom and properly educated entrepreneurs.

My endeavor here is bit of education and lot of choice.

Below is a a comment posted by a Linux user.

I accidentally stumbled upon while looking for now defunct Distromania.

"I used to think that the notion that there were too many Linux distros was overblown. Surely people could just pick one and use it. And, then there were all the horror stories of how difficult it was to install Linux. Not so, said I, installing Linux these days is just as easy – perhaps easier – than installing Windows. However, recently, I looked for a distro that would be suitable for a friend's old XP-based machine. That was when my pre-existing notions about Linux began to change…

Perhaps, I have been spoiled over the past few years by sticking to Ubuntu-type distros (Ubuntu with the Gnome Classic interface and, most recently, Mint with the Mate desktop). Typically, these install flawlessly, and work fairly well (although the raison d'être for this blog is essentially to document the fixes to problems that I encounter!).

However, the same cannot be said for all the distros out there.

My first foray into distro-world was Puppy Linux since this distro has a reputation for being a lightweight in terms of resource requirements, yet has a full slate of applications, and runs well on older hardware. What I couldn't initially figure out was how to establish a grub menu to dual-boot XP and Puppy. It turns out that there is a separate installation process for grub; however, while the main installation routine is under Setup in the main menu, grub's installer is under System!

Some even more challenging issues arose while trying a number of other distros. Macpup wouldn't run because the hardware didn't support PAE (Physical Address Extension) and Macpup no longer has a version with non-PAE kernel. Tiny Core Linux failed to install to the hard disk with the – unknown to Google – error message "Error mounting USB device". A strange error since I was installing from a CD-ROM. Damn Small Linux installed to the hard drive, said that it had installed grub, but failed to boot into a grub menu and loaded Windows. VectorLinux had an incomprehensible (to me) requirement to specify "run levels" and "services", and a very confusing set of selection buttons that seemed to be on when I thought they were off and vice-versa!

I could go on but, no doubt, you get the picture. For the non-Linux person – and even for some of us who know a little bit about Linux – finding, installing, and using an appropriate distro is not necessarily without its challenges."

Let me expand on this guy who pressed the "panic button", since I have used and tested more than 300 distributions.

His choices were pretty bad.

1. DML (Damn Small Linux) with only 50 MiB is only for the experts who work on terminals.

2. Vector Linux is a light weight dedicated Linux distribution for one who has some understanding about Linux programming.

It should be used alone in a single computer (like me who had 10 computers in a home network, running various Linux distributions. I have now dismantled all but one to cut down on my electricity bill) and for a Linux fanatic (like me) not for an ordinary user.

I must say I did not like it very much.

It is in the same fold as Absolute Linux (which has Gambase programming Language) but less versatile.

Puppy Linux my favorite since it is in my front pocket as a Mini CD or around my neck as a Flash Drive or in my smart phone as a mini SD (pull out, shove it into the SD card bay or into a USB bay and use it in an emergency) especially when I go abroad (as at present SD card with a mini operating system is unable to boot a smart phone and I hope it would be possible soon).

I use the smart phone as a bay or storage space.

I use Puppy Linux to test a new computer, I may think of buying on a schedule abroad (give it as a present or use it myself) and is only for an expert and not for a casual user.

That is why I published a book called "Teeny Weeny Linux".

So this guy is a spoiled guy trying to spoil another or scare another zombie.

My intention here is to make Linux "Fun and Game" and not a dreary exercise. That is why there are so many Live CD/ DVDs to play with. Installing is a different ball game, especially dual booting which I have adequately dealt with in my tiny book "Introduction to Linux".

I have now come to the conclusion that web is not the place to learn Linux and the web has become an easy portal to vent some steam and anger.

We used to call it the "Flame Wars" and it is not the trademark of a smart Linux user or a developer of present generation. It has become more academic and informative exercise currently, and the init and systemd are classic examples, I have made a little reference elsewhere in this book.

The wrong way using the right thing.

Get it right the first time is the classic statement in "Quality Management".

Chapter 02

Unifying all Linux Distributions

Is there a justifiable case for this approach?

Let me be forthright.

There is no case for Free software Foundation or the Community based Linux Distributions to follow a unifying theory.

In fact, it is a waste of productive human endeavour.

Just as there are many newspapers, and many models of cars and sports and clubs that deal with these sports institutions, the variety of Linux distributions deliver, a product that would appeal to a wider user base.

What is probably lacking in many developers' repertoire is that they do not focus on a particular theme or certain line of vision.

They do it for the fun of it.

It may have a religious flavour to begin with or a sportsman like or hobby type enthusiasm.

In that scenario, it is the human nature for the enthusiasm to wax and wane, especially of the community that helps to develop it. That is the very reason some of these distributions go into a dormant phase or hibernation.

Only a few of them have an ongoing active community support. The community support and their vigor is the one that make the Linux distributions successful.

It may not be true for a business model which is based on a particular task. Of course the business model tries to make ends meet and make a profit at the end of the day.

If one compares this with Fedora and Redhat, I believe that middle ground is never reached.

The tendency is for it to shift towards the business model.

They were the failures.

Suse also come into this fold and became a failure towards the end and sold the business interests.

For argument sake I will use five categories of users.

1. General users.
2. Hobbyist and Gamers.
3. Students.
4. Scientists.
5. Technocrats

The beauty of Linux is that it can cater for any of these appeals.

Unlike a business model which identifies, a certain section of the user population, a Linux distribution should not restrict itself to a certain segment of the users.

In the beginning of the Linux story and history it was the hobbyist that played the major role.

Now that Ubuntu has taken a very distinctive an admirable change of vision and direction other developers also should focus on these efforts with their own vision as a top priority.

I always say even Linux developers have to make room for providing rice and curry or bread and butter for their families. Once the hobby element is taken out of the denominator, the tendency is to focus on the real word economics, politics and domestic responsibilities.

One should not measure the success by the fan base.

It should be based on the utility value.

I will give one example since I have downloaded and tested as many as 300 hundred distributions from September, 2009 and still continue to do that with a less aggressive manner to cut down on my electricity bill and also because the Sri-Lankan Telecoms does not provide me the speed I pay them as a rental.

I pay for 50 K bit and get barely 5 K bit per second.

With the 20/20 promotion they only worry about the profit and not the service that they provide to their customers.

There was a distribution based on Slakware for writers and its last version was in 2009.

If I remember right it was named PocketWriter.

It was a live distribution and I could not install it on my computer. This was the time I was getting into the habit of writing a little note, at least to document Linux distributions briefly, a portion of the lovely distributions, I tested (not all).

I really liked this distribution.

This distribution has gone dormant since there are fewer writers in this world than readers.

I hope the developer who did this distribution if he reads this piece activate this distribution for the sake of writers like me.

That is the point I want to emphasize in this book.

Even though, the user base is limited the utility value of all the big and small Linux distributions outweighs the consumer base.

If we use the Unifying Theory we are going to lose these innovative but very useful distributions.

Some of them are tiny like Puppy, 4M Linux, Finnix and many more.

They have a place in this Universe of Linux distributions.

We must not fall into the trap of Apple and Windows mentality.

Now that I have tested few Apple Macs, it is pain in the neck for users like me who do not like to be slaves of the gadget as well as the operating system.

I hope I have now started a "Flame War".

It is good for the next generation of Linux distributions.

I hope somebody makes a distribution like PocketWrier for writers like me that can be installed in the netbook / laptop and not in a Super Computer.

That vision is lacking in Commercial and Corporate Linux. We need technocrats not the corporate CEOs.

This book is written to keep the spirit of Linux alive and the baton that takes the Linux message to change hand.

Then give a little push and say loudly Go, the moment one releases the baton!

The baton should not go in and endless private cycle or community but from place to place from one country to another until it reaches the far corners of this globe.

Chapter 03

Criteria for defining Suitability of Linux Distributions

With Gnome 3 and Kernel 3 in the horizon and tablet in the market and Ubuntu making a radical changes to desktop with Unity already arrived, I have decided to award a point scheme for all the distributions active now and write an update for all the Linux distributions I have downloaded so far.

That means moment, I post an update on a distribution, my old writing here in the blog post (Linux-100) probably become obsolete and would be taken out without prior notice.

I would be grateful if you post any errors of omission or commission on those post already here.

That means future posting will be slow to come and try my best to avoid any errors.

I will keep the total point given to each distribution (my own point scheme) close to my heart for the moment and won't publish them here.

I would elaborate on the points scored, later for sake of the completeness.

Points are given on quantitative as well as qualitative reasons.

Lowest mark is 10 and the highest mark is 300.

For an example I give 10 marks if it is only in French and 100 marks for multi-language capability. I will give 300 marks if it includes Sinhala / Tamil with its multi-language capability.

Similarly Ubuntu Unity gets 300 for its innovative approach and as a teaser for loyal fans who hate the new approach. I would include the total points for the old version as well as the new version.

This analysis is with desktop users in mind and server editions won't get any additional marks but I would state that server is available.

I will start with Linux Mint, since it has O.E.M version, codecs version with minimal multimedia support and almost pure without any software infringements and the full version with additional software.

It is a complete desktop and laptop friendly and currently rank as the top most download at www.distrowatch.com.

It has both 32 and 64 bit versions.

I am going to stop stating that PCLinux is the Gold Standard of live CD to eliminate my personnel bias on that distribution but have a Hypothetical Gold Standard defined by criteria below and with a point award of 2500.

So anything that approaches 2200 for CD version and above is potential Gold Standard and you are free to try it.

Nobody will get 100% assuming that no distribution has reached its peak and would be trying to achieve that goal with constant improvement and bug fixes.

For DVD the point award is 3500 points and anything that tops 3000 is a good value for money with 90% to 95% of all software included in the DVD.

I am a believer that "Small is Beautiful" and would figure out a way to award points and my guess is Puppy will come on top but there are equally good small utilities like SliTaz, 4MLinux, gParted and pMagic.

You are welcome to critically analyze my future writing with feedback but there is no attempt to compare with Microsoft and Apple Mac and in the next 5 to 10 years Linux will be way ahead of both of these distributions and I am not the one who need any pep commercial talks. In this period of course Linux guys and girls have to make 1000 and 1000 of tiny games and blockbuster games to invade the market in style.

They are already there on mobile phones and they have to mature with the hardware specially tablets in mind.

Criteria

A. Use

1. Live CD installable

2. Lightweight

3. Mini to LXDE to Standard

B. Internet

4. Easy Access to Internet

5. Automatically Configure Internet

6. Browser (ideally Firefox) Capability

7. Other browsers - Points for each additional browser

8. Email Capability-Thunderbird

9. Google gadgets but not essential

10. Torrent Down Loader

11. Skype or an alternative

12. Cloud-Dropbox

13. Cloud Other

C. Productivity

14. Office Package -Abiword

15. Office Package - Open office or Libre Office

16. Office Package - PDF Reader

17. Scribus

18. CD burner (ideally K3B)

19. CD burner (points for additional burners)

20. LightScribe/LaCie

D. Graphic

21. GIMP

22. Blender

23. Inkscape

24. Digicam

25. Tuxpaint

26. Special Graphics

27. Others

E. Audio

28. Mixer

29. Alsa

30. Others

F. Video

31. Imagination

32. VLC Player

33. Miro Internet TV

34. Cheese

35. TV Card

36. Others

37. Media Players including ability to play itunes and divx

G. Essential Utilities

38. Stable Grub Configuration

39. Partitioning tool is essential (ideally gParted)

40. Ability to clean up the temporary file at boot up

41. Updates and Package management

H. Archiving

42. Ark

43. File Roller

I. Children Programs

44. Light Weight Games

45. Children Version

46. Gcompris

J. Subjective

47. Reliability (most of them are)

48. Speed at start up (most of them are slow except YOPER)

49. Quick installation

50. Portability

51. Type of Desktops (Genome/KDE/LXDE)

52. Down loader that start from where one has left / stopped earlier

53. On line updates

54. Infrequent Cycles of Change

55. Downloads available for Libre Office,Open office, Skype

56. Speed at Start Up

K. Linux Fundamentals

57. Separate administrator in addition to normal user

58. Reliable Package Manager

59. Multi-Language in addition to English

60. Sinhala / Tamil Language Capability

61. Terminal

L. USB Boot Up

62. UnetBootIn

63. USB Creator

64. Live CD creator

M. Emulators

65. DOS

66. Wine

67. Oracle VM

68. Apple Emulation

N. Games

69. Light Weight

70. Advanced Games

O. Educational

71. Google Map

72. Tux Guitar

73. Tux Maths

P. Special and Development Utilities

74. Gambase

75. Web editor

76. PHP Admin

77. Scientific packages like statistics

Q. Access to Information

78. Home Web Site

79. Essential information including installation password etc

80. The facility for registration and writing reviews

R. Special Attributes

81. Less than 50 MiB

82. Less than 200 MiB

83. Less then 500 MiB

84. Innovative approach GOBO and YOPER

S. Finances and Printing

85. Gnumeric

86. GnuCash

87. Printing

T. Very Special

88. Religion

89. Language

90. Kernel Version

91. Version Number

92. New Desktop Type

93. Innovative Changes

94. 32 bits only

95. Both 32 and 64 bits

96. O.E.M.Version

97. ORCAS-Visually Handicapped

98. Home Page with Reviews

99. Distrowatch with Reviews

100. Softpedia Linux with Reviews

Chapter 04

10 (Ten) things a Linux Guy or Girl should do

Ten things a Linux Guy or Girl should do to become a geek and show off he is becoming a new groovy (I have coined this word in the same tone as savvy).

1. Linux Guy (means both s / he) should be able boot at any moment day or night. Should be able to boot out or weed out Linux of Microsoft as soon as possible (any dual facility of booting is taken as sign of weakness or of transvestism).

2. Should be able to root at any moment especially at night to look at the nocturnal misbehavior of a server platform or your computer.

3. Should be able to flame a war with any vendor who is dishing out and venturing into virtues of New Windows 7 (which is few years old anyway).

4. Should be able to flame a war with any neighbor who is using any Windows without a screen cover. All windows should have curtain cover so that you should not be seeing what your neighbor's daughter is doing or is up to.

5. Should carry a mini (business type) card or a Pendrive with at least Puppy Linux or Knoppix installed (this is a new addition to becoming a savvy-carry minimum of luggage in person).

6. Should have an old computer resurrected from the attic and used as a mail server educating newbies and flaming them with fire if they cannot boot or root instantaneously or as a dedicated seeding plot (seed potato type to germinate at any given time and not as a Microsoft couch potato type) storing at least 20 to 30 hacked (means used many times) distributions for dissemination by K-torrent running 24 / 7 schedule.

7. Should advocate running the computer 24 hours a day non stop (for seeding distributions to natives hitherto unknown with pidgin languages) for doing Cron jobs with midnight commander. If you tell this to a Microsoft Guy / Girl s/he will get a heart attack or they will be doing virus checking every half an hour.

8. Should be able to do short cuts with any combination of all 12 x F (function) Keys, Tab, Alt, Ctr. Shift (should never use the window key even with a sterile screen on top of it-why the hell it is there I still do not know in the key board) and any other alphanumeric key to do a simple jobs not understood by a kid or a newbie.

When you do that with the last touch of the key on F-12, a word presto should pop out for a second and a pause and then ask what next please (really you should write a mini shell script for above and assign it to the 12th Function Key nobody seems to be using it nowadays).

Linux never extended it beyond 8 Function Keys in my time.

Or else you must design a few Cron jobs yourself and assign them to F-9 to F-12

If nobody is impressed, at least your girl friend or boy friend will be impressed by this activity.

9. Should be able to work with virtual keyboard even when the normal keyboard has coffee or tea spilled all over it by a kid while watching your antics.

10. This is a new one again since Microsofties think that Linux guy cannot play games. You must use the guitaristX (new distribution in Linux) key to play a game or two while stringing some music with John Lenon or Paul McCartney in in the background.

11. This is an extra for a Sri-Lankan guy to show off that you can do Linux now in Sinhala and that is you say "You are an Eternally Distressed-Distro-Hopper".

You like plain hoppers, egg hoppers, Linux hoppers, jaggery hoppers or hoppers from heaven (in any case it looks like food is coming down from heaven when one look at the prices).

Important

I have now with me all the Debian (386) Live and Installable CDs / DVDs for spreading the message of Linux in Sinhala. It can be installed in Tamil, Telangu and English too for Linux Lovers in the Indian Subcontinent.

It also has 64 bit version.

I would initiate a mechanism to make them available initially in Kandy and the University where I work does not permit me to access public directly.

Please log at this particular writing and make some comments.

There is another alternative to Drop them at Droppbox but that will be lot of work for me.

A paper advertisement is an alternative.

Please do not contact me (no emails accepted) other than this portal.

PS

This was posted many moons ago!

Chapter 05

Ten (10) Plus points about Linux Distributions when in Use

It is time, I should write some important things about Linux that you may not read in books but only experienced regular user will tell you.

Even though, most of the proprietary guys do not provide the necessary drivers for Linux or support Linux, the modules that are used in new kernels are robust and reliable and never fail. They look after the hardware without breaking them down even if you use the system 24 /7 schedule unlike Microsoft counterparts.

Linux kernel is made to run 24 / 7 schedule without braking down (except normal maintenance). The maintenance jobs are done in the early hours of the day (they are called CRON jobs) when system is not in use but with idling and with power on. One of the biggest mistakes Linux newbies do is to switch off the computer in the night. Unfortunately running 24 hours is not practiced in our university setup since by evening and over weekends servers are switched off and junk that should have been removed automatically get collected, overnight and over the weekend.

1. One is able to run your computer 24 / 7 schedule is its strongest point and its strength. No need for restarts every time a minor configuration change is made unlike in windows. These changes are done in real time and no delay is contemplated, the moment a command is activated.

2. Linux look after the time scheduling to nanoseconds. For example if one is using K-torrents for downloading several files, it shares time allotment with the files. Faster files get a bigger share and slower files get a smaller share and the full band width is used. One can limit the upload and download speeds if it is used in a network.

3. Looks after the hardware and the processor well and if there are problems they are reported at boot time (one should be able to read these messages at boot time which are displaced for a fraction of a second). Once a major problem is detected the Linux has the canny habit of switching off instantaneously.

Once after a lightening and power outage (it ran through even the UPS battery) one of my computers had some electrical burns. The system never ran more than few seconds after this power outage, for me to read the error message. After three days only I realized the problem but it had been telling me that the cooling had gone wrong on the first few seconds which I was not able to read fast enough. This problem was solved with the help of a young guy but I was all the time thinking of a boot virus since I fixed a second hand Sata hard disk 3 days before to up the capacity. Linux boot and grub file have a good warning systems, if one is careful to read them at boot time.

Not only Linux is a work horse it looks after minor injuries to the horse.

4. What I really like about Linux is it looks after CD ROMs and CD/DVD writers well. It usually run on default setup but at write time it tests both the CD/DVD and uses the best and safe formula and writes the job in incremental or decremental speed. It does not start writing even if there is a minor fault in the CD or DVD. It does not do a job blindly, it assesses the process and resources even to mini seconds. One little advice here. If your RAM is 1 GiB or less do not run torrent when disk burner is used. It allocates more RAM (memory) for the torrent and CD burner might ground to a halt.

5. It is really a multitasking Operating System unlike Windows and work with other computers in a network and synchronize work.

6. It is multiuser operating system (Ubuntu lacks this due to changes to the desktop system and that is one of my reasons not favoring it in spite of the wider user base).

7. It records (keeps a history) and everything is measured to nanoseconds.

8. It uses RAM efficiently and when things are not favorable uses SWAP partition (not swap file as in Windows) to swap files and data. This is why it is much efficient than Windows.

9. It is secure from attack if the firewall is properly configured and it is almost free of viruses.

10. It keeps everything in a designated place and file structure is stable even though rigid and your data is in (need to be partitioned accordingly) a home partition. I can upgrade or reinstall the system without any changes to the home (data) partition. That was one reason I really liked it when I was testing many distributions in the early days of my Linux adventure.

I have never lost a file for 15 years.

Would you believe it?

Only problem is now I am short of short term memory and I forget with what name I had named a particular file. I have downloaded over three (300) hundred images and made mistakes in only 3 out of the first 100 and nothing after that.

It is almost zero after I started using K-torrent.

If you want a work horse to do your jobs.

It is always Linux.

I will come back with minor nuances of Linux sometime later.

I am happy to report that Debian 6 (now 8) is available with Sinhala graphical installer.

Chapter 06

Final Count Down on Linux 100

December 12th 2011

I am almost completing 18 months come end of March of downloading and testing Linux Live CDs and lately few of the DVDs.

All good things have to come to an end and with Sinhala Linux coming to the scene without fanfare or funfair after a long delay, I will be concentrating on that instead of the Live CDs but with occasional reference to them (not full time as it used to be for nearly 18 months).

Real reason for this venture was the boring one year election campaign and as a diversion tactics of an intellectual nature.

The things I learned was enormous.

Sinhala Linux coming at the tail end was quite a surprise.

It looks as some of my critical comments are taken with serious attention and lot of my audience is not Sri-Lankans but Americans and far away web browsers.

I believe my comments were only academic and may be some times constructive but lot of things not intended by me has / have happened.

In the Grand Finale, I would like to list few.

Summary

1. Multilingual Distributions are coming from EU and South America which is pretty good.

2. French is also becoming a leading language of distributions.

3. Light weight and multiple editions are hitting the bench, emulating PCLimux, Sabayon (Gentoo), Salix (Slackware), Aptosid (Debain), Fedora (Redhat) and Zenwalk are examples.

4. Some dormant like Korora coming out of the attic.

5. Distributions are looking at others to emulate or improve the Linux image.

6. Dominance of Ubuntu is diminishing and Ubuntu also looking for an image lift.

7. Redhat has come out of hibernation.

8. Debian is showing its prowess and slowly and rightly embracing the changes. Lot of live editions including Sinhala Linux edition.

9. Flame wars are becoming less intense but critical and constructive.

10. With all these I am becoming rejuvenated at my twilight years.

The old and young are coming together for a Grand Finale.

11. Puppy (front pocket) and Knoppix (piggyback) remain my favorites.

12. Pendrive Linux are ubiquitous.

Only criticism I have is the children programs (except gCompris and few others) and games have been neglected.

Morphix, Myah and Adios are slow to wake up from hibernation or slumber.

Young chaps take them out of the attic and put some grandpa influence on the map and make some really grandiose games and creative activities (for children and grandpa like me) and reinvigorate the Linux spirit of the yesteryear.

Chapter 07

Note sent to a newbie in Linux

Down below is a note I sent to a young newbie.

Two (2) GiB is enough (not for graphic intensive windows games) for Linux except for games.

I have only one (1) GiB (4 GiB in my laptop which I use only for testing occasionally) in my old computer.

It is a waste of money going for more RAM with very slow Internet in Sri-Lanka.

I only use K-Torrents now and it is currently downloading at less than 5 KB/sec .

Solution is for having at least two / three computers.

1. One for Games and Videos

2. Simple secondhand computer with Linux for Internet (can share with your sister or brother and family members).

3. Netbook with Android when you enter University (not now).

Except my laptop and my daughters netbook all the computers at home are very good secondhand IBM computers (cost less than Rs.20,000/= with little upgrading of the RAM but not graphic cards).

Secondhand desktops are good buys if you understand the hardware and look at inside before buying.

I test them with my Linux CD/DVDs before buying and there are lot of Linux utilities to test and Linux will work day and night for 10 years.

None of my computers broke down after I started using Linux (before that 3 new computers on Windows) except one graphic card and a few RAM cards in the learning stage.

They work 24/7 schedule and the UPS battery is very important.

This is one reason I promote Linux and I do not fear viruses now.

Only down side is Games with Linux which I will probably concentrate when I retire and nothing else to do.

I have two game DVDs but I will not give it to anybody since Linux is for real and serious computing and not for games and leisure! Never buy a secondhand laptop or netbook. Wait till new models come and with long battery life and you need it in the university and the government is unable to pay dons and do not expect them to help you with computers (not in Singapore though) when you eventually enter University.

Just look at the versatility of Linux.

1. Linux powers international space stations

2. Linux powers the technology in Cadillac cars

3. Linux powers air traffic control systems

4. Google, Facebook, Twitter, all use Linux

5. 9 out of 10 supercomputers in the world run on Linux

Chapter 08

From Teacher to a Student (hypothetical)

Learning Linux is easy if you take one step at a time.

When I started there was nobody to guide me.

I used to read books (This is where English is important) and very fast.

That is a technique (reading fast and also digesting the material) I developed on my own. Give me any big book I will read (not from cover to cover) only what I want, that is also to solve a problem (for example installing Linux) and pick up the important things in 3 to 4 days.

This is something essential in higher studies.

One does not read for the sake of reading in science (reading in other fields including philosophy is different).

One focus on why one reads this or that and make one's own personal assessment in the course of the reading.

Early days I used to get bogged down in two or three days without any progress.

Then I take a break and think about the problem deep and somehow get to the point (D.I.Y - Do It Yourself) where I want to make progress.

It naturally comes.

We all have this natural ability but examinations do not make us better but show where we are weak.

After every examination we have to go for a higher level and a more difficult level.

Even though A Level is difficult we make life easy after the 1st year Examination. Unfortunately 1st year examination is the most difficult for all.

The poor English skills compounds the difficulty.

This is especially so in Maths and IT.

Maths is difficult if one is not in it.

I was very good in my maths including applied mathematics and used to beat all in my class.

Then one day, I decided to go for biology for no particular reason (the speed of reading was a bonus) and without any help covered the syllabus myself (D.I.Y).

Rest was history and I never felt big but looked for the next challenge.

When you get bogged down in a mathematical problem do not try to solve it by somehow.

Think, analyze and look at the problem in a different way.

There is always several ways of solving problems and try to grasp the concept.

What I found in the university setup when teaching was students struggle to grasp the key points and concepts.

Not like in the old days.

I do not know why?

Other problem is they cannot read a manual and follow instructions according to the manual and its instructions.

This is where reading is important.

So concentrate on your Mathematics and English.

Rest will follow.

Take Linux as a problem and a hobby to take a break from your studies.

Do not make it your first interest.

But keep trying and look at where you go wrong.

This talent is essential in IT.

There is something called fixing bugs.

This is where both mathematical concepts and programming merge.

Even though, I do not write programs, I am good looking at bugs. In private sector setting with number of programmers working on a Unix database, I used to tease them with complex queries, for them to find a solution for a given problem.

That probably has come from my analytical skills learned from pathology.

Try to be a problem analyst.

The term in IT is system analyst.

If a server breaks down one has to find where and when and what has gone wrong?

Without trying to spoon feed, I have given here a list or the methods that I have used to solve a given problem not necessarily in Linux but in real life situation.

One or two method/s is/are enough at an examination but in teaching (as a teacher I have to cater for students with different skills and no two are the same in my assessment) one has to look at the global picture and focus on different aspects of a problem.

That is the difference between a student and a teacher.

It is sometimes very hard to become a good teacher.

If I am given a chance I prefer to be a student.

That is where I always enjoyed.

But having to teach a brighter student is a blessing.

Linus Torvald, I like him the most because he showed that his professor was wrong.

There are many ways to solve a given problem.

Not only the professor's given method.

This is how the business world operate and there are Teams and not Lords.

Chapter 09

Ten or more steps of my own

I have taken some bold steps (decisions) in my life from my childhood and that had come good, when I reflect on them. Some of them cannot be mentioned here.

I was a keen observer of nature and people around me and learned to be bold and fearless.

Most of my teachers except who taught me Sinhala and English were mediocre.

I often wondered how they ever became teachers especially in science.

1. One bold step was not to believe teachers especially in science.

That was a very scientific decision by itself.

I had the knack and keen power of observation and problem solving ability. For example, I believed anything can be grown on our soil, be that it may be, seeds or yam or runner provided I water them regularly. My father was not a farmer but he was a keen gardener (which he learned from a burger gentleman).

Except potatoes, I could do that on my own but could not figure out why I could not grow potatoes (those days potatoes came from UK and I did not know that they put chemicals to inhibit sprouting and made sure seed potatoes were never given to us. I discovered this many many years later. This is how western countries help us).

2. I decided never to ask scientific questions (why potatoes could not grow) from my teachers (knowing very well they will give a wrong answer to shut my mouth).

3. I decided to do science and one day I decided not to go to the school I was attending abruptly (there were many reasons) and that was a very bold decision. Finding a school teaching science was difficult, but I eventually found one but it did not have able bodies to teach science.

4. I decided not to proceed with cadetting even though, I was the leader in my old school (I was thrashed by the teacher / principal three times in the new school but I stood my ground).

I took part in all other sports except cadettting (reason should be obvious and there is / was a worse form of ragging which included sexual for the young).

5. New school was no better in teaching science and I made the decision to do D.I.Y learning science (thank god there were two Foreign libraries outside the school, stocked with old science books in Kandy then).

6. Due to harassing by teachers, I decided to walk out of the science class and asked permission from the principal who thrashed me for not joining cadets.

He eventually acceded (I still thank him for that help) to my demand (man with military training) knowing my will power.

Little he knew that others will join me later.

7. We decided to work towards a common (first exercise in group work) goal and enter university in the first attempt (both Bio and Maths).

Eventually, all of us did pass and none from the class who attended normal class did.

They thought we (me especially) had gone bonkers.

8. Next decision was to get rid of all the science teachers in one go and get some decent ones. By this time I have forged some connections with science school inspector who was very helpful.

Proof of the pudding was that nobody from the normal class passed.

Some teachers feared me more than the principal and I was not a good cohort for them.

9. We never went for tuition classes and we never got involved in giving tuition to others except my cousin brother who eventually became an engineer.

He failed all his subjects in "O" Level and till he entered the university he was under my clutches.

10. Next decision was to get rid of the compulsory government service act that we had to serve (IMF would love this) for six years and never to join the government service except the university (semi-autonomous institution and not a government per say).

The way things are happening and developing in the university now leaving that is also not a big decision for me.

Rest that followed is history.

I suppose nobody should try these methods now since all the systems including schools in this country are very poorly managed by over 100 of ministers and ministries.

There is no half way house for us now as the saying in English goes.

You may wonder why I included this as a chapter.

Recently we had a party at home and we had a discussion with a group of people nearing fifty.

I asked a leading question to divert them from a mundane political talk.

I asked them what were their childhood aspirations and why they failed to reach the goal post.

Unanimous agreement was that the teachers were terrors (better term terrorists) themselves and they were very poor teachers.

Then I retorted why didn't they become assertive like me.

There was no response since time had lapsed when they realized they were under wrong guides.

The decision we made was to bring this to focus and make it a discussion topic.

They answer was not rush to tuition classes but get the system works for you better and right now.

So this intrusion on Linux box/book is equally valid.

If somebody says you cannot learn Linux, prove him otherwise by your own hard work.

Chapter 10

Tablets is going to make print media obsolete

Why talk about tablets and smart phone in a book on Linux?

Is it out of place?

I think smart phone in particular is the biggest threat to Linux base. There will be be more and more people using smart phones instead of desktop computers.

A smart phone is actually a mini computer.

The tablet with phone is just a big version and people will be using it, only as a basic communication gadget but not as a mini computer.

That is my reasoning.

1. I think print might disappear giving way to digital news.

2. Unlike the print paper, it can read you the news, while you drive your car.

3. Local Paper edition might come in smart cards.

4. Advertisement supplements in the digital format will make one to order with the touch of your finger tips.

5. Sports can be live like in the TV but unlike TV you can replay the match or game you like.

6. It has audio and video capabilities.

7. Even Amazon is going to phase out E-Reader and go for Tablets.

8. All these are due to Linux and Android entering the market.

It is a reality and not futuristic.

9. Tablet is your News Reader, E-Reader, the smart phone, the web browser and the travel companion.

10. This is why I support Unity and very soon Google's Android with Linux operating system will overtake the Apple's iPod, since they are going to market it at an affordable price.

11. Not only that, smart news papers magnets will dish out OEM version of Tabloid at cut price with their subscription attached to the deal.

In the next 10 years we are going to see amazing changes in the West.

I do not see these changes will come true in this part of the world where professors in IT industry has to go behind politicians in begging bowl for his or her salary increase.

The promise of giving computers to university on loan will be a wasteful exercise and students drawn into debt no sooner they enter higher education. If you are a smart student one should not go into debt buying a laptop before Tablets hit the market.

If you do so, you might have to be in debt for two items instead of one.

Why I won't buy a Tablet soon?

Tablets are going to take all us by surprise and when it hits the market and the price is right everybody will join the band wagon.

1. It is light in weight.

2. It is mobile smart phone.

3. It has a touch screen.

4. It is the news reader.

5. It is the web browser.

6. It is in every C.E.O.'s hand

7. Unlike the paper it will read the news while you drive the car.

8. It is the E-reader

9. Business companion, stock dealer and buying machine on E-bay and Stock Market

10. Sports can be live like in the TV but unlike TV you can replay the match or game you like.

All these fancy features make the yuppies to go for it and the rest will follow.

That is what the predictions are.

But I won't buy one in a hurry.

I need the following conditions satisfied.

1. It should have an alarm or a siren attached to it as in the car doors.

Why?

Like laptops, mobiles and money it is the item everybody wants to steal.

2. It should have pass word protection.

Why?

If it is stolen the thief (unless he is a hacker) should not be able to use it and the user should be able to track it down.

3. It should have a location mapper or a tag which we put on dogs.

Why ?

To locate it, if misplaced.

4. It should have a long life battery.

5. It should have solar panel.

Why?

In countries like us where electricity price is exorbitant and on Sunny days when we have power cuts, this is the only fun we can have outdoors.

6. It should have satellite (not 3G or 4G version) communication facility.

Why?

In countries like us where the Telecoms never give the band width they promise us and we pay for, this is the only way we can tune into America and A.O.L

7. It should have at least 4 USB ports, if not new ports with ability to expand it to a switch or a plug.

Just like raspberry-pi mini computer.

The above points are general purpose and below are my own specifications.

8. Big hard drive with ability to put my own Lightweight Linux Distributions instead of Android only and dual boot it.

9. Ability to boot up with my Pendrive, if the above cannot be allowed due to Company Law.

10. Ten is the most important one.

Sturdy titanium case shock proof.

Why?

If Android does not work the way, I want it to work, I want to thrash it on the floor and see how it survives or works.

If it does, I will appear free on a commercial for Google.

There is another reason.

I was one who supported Google from the very beginning when they announced it, many moons ago and remained solid with it due to Linux capabilities and they did not invite me for the party and also did not give me a free version to test.

11. Real reason, I do not want to go for the tablet is, the lack of good and easy keyboard but ASUS has changed this radically by adding a transformer / converter to the tablet.

12. All American car manufacturers should install a tablet in the dashboard with appropriate buttons to listen to music, TV and newspaper .

Why?

This way we can prevent lot of road accidents, even in the the 3rd world and the big Americans can say they were the pioneers of prevention of road accidents.

Apart from all those real or perceived reasons, anything that attempts to kill Linux or Free Software Foundation, I get activated by default.

This is why I supported Unity of Ubuntu and its phone but sadly they have given up on the phone.

Chapter 11

Linux-100

I have over 200 distributions and images stored all over my hard disks and CDs and DVDs and I continue to download at least a few more of them a week to test.

My search for (looking for) best hundred has being of no avail. It is time for me to do it myself for the benefit of Linux fans and newbies.

Internet has being immensely helpful.

First of all I must thank the guys / girls of the following non-commercial and few commercial sources.

Number one goes to Distromania.com (unfortunately it is no longer in existence) since they keep a catalog of old distributions and also list the new and latest distributions.

Distrowatch.com also doing a good job of it but unfortunately they seem to miss some of the old ones.

Softpedia com has enormous number of pages and like Distrowatch.com do not keep a repository of old distribution images and their links.

Linux online also list distribution in their site.

Linux Live CD list is the only one which list the distributions according to to the types, education, games. desktop, multimedia. science, medicine etc.

I recommend this site for anybody who is choosy for a particular type say for kids, education.

Elive for at least releasing the development version free.

There are many more and thanks to all of them.

Couple of years ago the story was different one had to browse or read a Linux Bible to gather information, Now these guys who write books do not bother to update them since the updating task is extremely difficult due to the rapid pace at which Linux is moving.

Only a rocket scientist can keep pace with.

My attempt is to fill this void albeit in smaller doses.

I thought of using a bit of scientific approach using my own criteria.

My criteria are based the practical difficulties, we face in this country due to poor (comparatively better compared to India but no where near the capabilities of Singapore), Internet Service and download speed.

It is practically impossible to download a DVD more than 1 GiB.

It takes ages even for that.

So I have concentrated on CD rather than DVDs.

My impression, it is better for us to have number of CDs rather than DVDs.

I used to download up to 7 Debian CDs in the past when I had only Redhat and Mandriva.

To decide my 100 Linux distributions of choice I will use many criteria.

My Criteria

1. Live CD which can be installed on hard disk 25 points

2. Easy access to Internet 20 points

3. Automatically Configure Internet 30 points

4. Browser (ideally Firefox) Capability 10 points

5. Other browsers 05 point

6. Google gadgets but not essential 10 points

7. Skype 15 points

8. Office Package (Abiword or Open office) 15 points

9. Light Weight (very important) 30 points

10. CD burner, very important (ideally K3B) 20 for K3B and 5 for others

11. Stable Grub configuration 30 points

12. Partitioning tool is essential (ideally gParted) 30 points

13. Light weight games 20 points

14. Ability to clean up the temporary file at boot up 50 points

15. Updates and Package Management 10 points

16. Reliability (most of them are) 50 points

17. Many versions form Mini to LXDE to Standard and Children's, 25 points for each

18. Speed at start up (most of them are slow except YOPER) 100 points

19. Quick installation 20 points

20. Multi-Language in addition to English 25 points

21. Separate administrator in addition to normal user 50 points

22. Digikam and Gimp 20 points

23. Media Players including ability to play itunes and divx 30 points

24. Type of Desktops (Genome / KDE/ Fluxbox) 25 points

25. Down loader that start from where one has left / stopped earlier 50 points

26. Infrequent Cycles of Change (new distributions) but frequent updates 50 points

27. USB boot up 30 points

28. Live CD creator 20 points

29. Wine (Window emulation) 20 points

30. Apple Emulation 30 points

31. Innovative approach like GOBO and YOPER 100 points

32. Home web site and the facility for registration and writing reviews 100 points

33. Scientific packages like statistics 100 points

34. Blender (Maya equivalent) 200 points

35. Children Educational packages with games 300 points

I will start with Linux Mint, Gos 3.1-Gadgets and Berry to begin with, which is a cute one. Children educational packages I have given bonus marks since they should be developed as separate distributions such as youknow4kids, Knoppix for kids, Edbuntu, Qimo, Ubermix and Sugar on a Stick.

4th April, 2010

Chapter 12

1. Do you want, Simple, Fast and Elegant way to write?

The answer is not Microsoft but AbiWord.

Do you know the size of the executive file?

It is less than 8 MiB.

Plug in can be installed later if one needs it.

Do you want to do collaborative work online?

Perhaps in a school set up!

It is Abiword.

Do you know how much memory it uses for a blank document?

Below is is the breakdown on a Linux machine.

Type gmemusage in Terminal and one gets;

RAM allocations on my Debian desktop.

When opened to blank documents, OO uses 60 MiB of RAM.

Compared to 30 MiB for Abiword,

Compared to 8 MiB for Bluefish (Web Editor with graphics)

Vi uses the lowest memory when

On gmemusage output.

OO is a pig,

Abiword is an ant eater,

Bluefish is a minnow

Vi is the one on diet,

What is the Microsoft Word 2007 eating capacity?

It is a Gorilla Crashing on a dinner party (not G.O.P.).

I hear an Apple Guy saying that it takes Microsoft 10 minutes to work out the RAM load of 2 minutes of its use and opening up a blank document.

What about the Apple takes to open a word document?

I am told it is a trade secret they wish not or would not share with Microsoft or Linux guys and girls?

What if you got an email with an attachment of word 2007 and you are unable to open it?

1. Open AbiWord blank document.

2. Copy the Microsoft document with its Macros.

3. Paste in AbiWord without formatting

4. In seconds you have clear word document which you can edit and post it back to the sender with a note when you send an important messages shed all the dead weight or proprietary load which I am not prepared to stomach in on a busy Monday.

Why I write this?

Well when the tablets hit the market, they should use a strip down version of Abiword instead of a Microsoft's notepad.

Yes Source Code is available free and the particular distribution can add the necessary tit bits for its proper use.

Linux of course unlike 5 years ago have started incorporating Abiword in their distribution shedding dead weight of Open Office and adding more useful packages like UnetBootIn, Web Editor (Bluefish), CD/DVD burners and the likes.

Chapter 13

Incognito Linux and the Visually handicapped

This is something one should take cognizant of.

I was looking for a post in the name of incognito in my blogspot but I have posted it as Webbo Amnesia.

Amnesia is a medical term and I had gone to the town with that word and has completely forgotten to highlight the Linux distribution in my post.

My apologies to the guys and girls at Incognito.

The error of commission and omission should be put right here.

1. It is a Live CD if one wants to browse anonymously and without leaving any traces to detect.

2. It has vidalia which gives a list of guys logged in at the time of one's current browsing.

3. It has ORCAs which is something I should highlight here.

Even a blind person can browse the web without any intrusion or obstruction.

4. Web browser is light and no cookies or attempting to remember all one's actions.

5. It does not feed back your browsing habit to commercial interests. It is fast because of that fact and I was immediately on my blog entry and reading its first few lines.

I am happy even a blind person can read this entry if he/she accidentally visit my site. There are lot of nice Linux guys/girls out there doing things that are commendable.

Helping visually handicapped to be independent is one such thing.

Thanks a lot to all ORCAs developers out there.

Incognito is an amazing utility which all the aspiring politicians and power hungry ones should worry about. It can boot and erase all the traces of memory in the browser and the computer of use after posting a message out of the country which some dictators like what you find in China may not like, and the true state of affairs are known to the rest of the world.

Tor is a small utility one can carry in a floppy disk and it will send chills down the spines of some politicians!

Linux can do it and WWW is for all not for a few powerful and wealthy.

It makes the ground rules simple and open.

Be transparent in all public (not private) affairs.

What I gather is that this utility is used by teenagers in the West to hoodwink their parents and reach unwanted sites.

Well, teens are two steps ahead of their parents and old folks should fast learn "tricks of the trade".

Use of this utility in bad hands can be deplorable but I will use it only when there is a dire necessity political-wise.

1. Number one feature one I want all the Linux distribution to have is UnetBootIn.

2. Number two is ORCAs.

3. Number three is gParted and partition image.

Incognito has all three of it.

Knoppix has all three of it.

Most of the Ubuntu derivatives Vinux has it.

Dynabolic should have it and it has it.

The visually handicapped will enjoy Music with Dynabolic.

In other words all audio visual Linux CD/DVDs should have ORCAs and UnetBootIn.

So he/she can wear the distribution around the neck wherever they go.

Who knows I am in my twilight years and I may go blind due to old age and I will have to carry one with me.

Thanks young guys and girls for your wonderful communal spirit.

Chapter 14

Lot can go wrong with Android tablets.

Long period elapsed from the concept to execution and most of it was tested on high end of the market.

The average user was not involved in the decision making.

It was probably an effort of a small team which worked hard (dedicated to the task at hand).

To begin with it was the development of the browser.

Then the tiny OS without security enhancements.

It was a new browser not a time tested one.

There were many suitable candidates for this new browser in the Linux community and none of them were considered or compared with the Chrome.

Now take Firefox.

It has lot of loop holes when used in the Microsoft Environment.

It originated from Linux base but then arched its way out to embrace Microsoft community.

With that it lost the security features.

It is possible to customize it in the Linux environment and even in that environment some cookies till lately (penetrated even my computer) do some undesirable things.

I was doing lot of downloads without a firewall and hacker (most likely Windows guy from India-that is far as I went in search of the guy) installed a script in the browser.

Fortunately, I detected it in a matter of hours and took necessary steps.

Instead of point to point download, I went for Torrents which has a way of of using the port and testing the threads.

Even torrents can be attacked and it happened to LinuxTracker and lately Linux foundation is affected by a similar attack.

If Linux could be attacked it is going to be chicken feed for attackers in Microsoft environment.

Chrome will have to deal with this threat.

It has no human resource to deal with like in the Linux Community.

In a commercial environment Linux does not prosper as was shown in Fedora Project.

Fedora's contribution was marginal when compared to Debian.

It was only few day ago I (rather PCLinux) detected something fishy.

I was using point to point download overnight (two files) and one of them (either Zenwalk or Absolute Linux let in a cookie in between the download streams disrupting my download (point to point).

Equally it could have happened after the downloads were finished and I did not terminate the download as usual and left the computer running.

If I had the torrent running this would not have happened which I usually do.

I removed all the Google Cookies (including useful ones) to get some sanity back and system running smoothly.

Any browser is vulnerable and not foolhardy.

So Google gadgets are also vulnerable.

In any case I do not use Chrome.

I am into Cloud Computing, I have to and, I will be using browsers.

I think Linux has to develop a utility like torrent to deal with this problem and Google with its limited staff cannot do that.

For cloud to succeed something better than the browser has to take the tiny computing moments and events into control.

I believe the browser is not the best vehicle for Cloud computing.

Time will tell whether my apprehensions are true or false.

Google cannot do it alone.

The stakes are high if they fail.

Like viruses for Microsoft, it will be Cookies for Google that set in a bad omen (for Chrome and Google).

It has to forge a friendship with Linux Community for it to be successful.

The mistake it did was to declare it's kernel is pure and original.

It is not and it is vulnerable.

Linux has to look forward to the challenge and take a giant stride now (before it is too late) in Cloud Computing.

Linux can do it with or without Google's help.

That is my belief.

Chapter 15

F-Droid and Mobiles

F stand for freedom dishing out over 1500 open source packages that work on Androids.

It looks like, I have missed the bus as regard to the mobile world.

There is a reason for it.

Coming from Linux base, I even did not like Android since it became proprietary.

Like Microsoft it flooded the market leaving behind alternative Linux Operating systems, far behind.

Ubuntu failed in its crowd funding of the Mobile Phone but it has put out Ubuntu Touch which is the next best alternative OS, currently available.

I was hopeful on Firefox Os and its phone but it is going through the teething problems.

Replicant

There is Replicant of Gnome base that is making giant strides.

What is interesting of Replicant is, it has the wherewithal to crack a proprietary phone and install it instead.

It took a long time for the CyanogenMod come to roost.

Replicant is CyanogenMod minus proprietary components.

There is Sailfish but none of them could match the Android currently.

Using a Rootkit to crack a proprietary phone may be costly and one loses the warranty.

Until then we have F-Droid, F stand for freedom dishing out over 1500 open source packages that work on Androids.

As at present, the mobile is a mini computer.

One should have the freedom to use the way one uses a computer. I consider the mobile phone as a cloud client, almost all the Androids can be hacked and are vulnerable.

So vulnerability can be eliminated by using the cloud.

Mind you cloud also can be attacked.

To use the mobile as a cloud client we need a light weight browser.

I am glad to say there is one open source browser called Lightening which is faster than any currently available browsers.

I am bit rusty on all these issues but Linux Magazine is doing a great job by having very illuminating articles.

I hope they would do a magazine dedicated to Mobiles by December.

That is the time everybody thinks of a new mobile or or a spare one or a Tablet.

If you do so please make sure or demand them to provide you security packages / virus guards.

Chapter 16

Top 25 Linux Distributions

I have analyzed over 50 Linux distributions both qualitatively and quantitatively and following is a summary according to the points scored ad the top 10.

Rest are listed according to the points awarded without a comment.

Top Rank

1. Debian

Debian scored 3005 points.

Coming to IT industry where there are very few heroes Debian is the clear winner which gyrates and spins at the correct orbit.

It was no surprise.

Score of above 3000 and well above the Gold Standard of 2500 for the standard CD/DVD.

For the heavy weight category it is within the Gold Mark where no other distribution has all the components at disposal with over 60,000 package well tested and stable.

It has gParted which is around 100 MiB with partition tool and security features.

It has Blender, Scribus and Inkscape.

Only missing component was O.E.M. component.

2. Ultimate Linux

ArtistX

Ranking Second with 2620 points is Untimate Linux.

It is taking whopping 2620 points, simply because it's a games DVD based on Ubuntu and it has graphic features including Inkscape and Blender.

Apart from that it is basically a Ubuntu distribution.

Even though, it gets lot of points due to inclusion of many packages it should be used as a games DVD rather than a general purpose distribution.

This warning is due to the changes in Ubuntu Unity and the attendant repository changes that may ensue, as a result of that change.

It does not have LibreOffice but one can easily download it after installation.

I missed ArtistX and it scores almost the same points and vie for the second place.

3. UberStudent with 2610 points

The ranking number is 3.

This is one of the very good Ubuntu derivative packed with utilities. The utilities that I could not find included gParted, and Blender.

It's on the fat side with 2.7 GiB image.

This is one of the Linux distributions I could not download due to download problem but with some difficulty I managed to download both the CD and the DVD versions.

There were not enough seeders but I used the point to point download.

It's Ubuntu based and excellent for students in the higher grades and in the University. It has many utilities that student would like to use in literature search albeit web based.

I have no hesitation in recommending it.

It has almost everything one needs.

Why blender was not included is a bit of a mystery.

4. Knoppix

Knoppix fourth with 2410 / (GnuArtist 2445).

Knoppix stands tall and scores 2410 which is well above Ubuntu and Unity on the threshold of becoming a Gold Standard on its own.

It is 4th in the my list of 50 and only three others above.

Debian comes first.

Ultimate Linux comes second.

UberStudent comes third. Packed with utilities except Blender and gParted.

Good old days when it was difficult to find a distribution and DEMO CDs were hard to come by Knoppix started the revolution of Live CDs.

I have used it from its 3.1 version and up and it was available even in Sri-Lanka.

Its significant features apart from Live CD running on RAM are;

1. Good hardware detection

2. Sound configuration and unique start up with sound effects.

3. Ability to compress lot of programs into a CD/DVD.

4. Enormous number of packages.

5. Partition tool and many more.

6. ORCAs that is fun for visually handicapped user and is as good as Vinux which supports visually handicapped user.

It was way ahead until Puppy Linux came into the scene and took another twist by making Live CD under 100 MiB.

Soon, I became a convert of Puppy Linux with the inherent tendency in me, the love for the canine species.

Its weakness was it could not be installed into the hard disk and I found a way to mount it on a FAT partition. I always had a copy mounted on my hard disk when the LXDE came into the scene.

Then came the 10th anniversary release of Knoppix which was a big hit by itself both CD and DVD versions with the ability to install into the hard disk. It allowed administrative rights after installing to secure one's data. The restoring of administrative right was a welcome change for the ardent Linux users. The live Linux sessions disregarded the built in right of the root user. This came handy if for some reason you forgot the root password of a distribution and one could not recover one's own data and documents.

There is Knoppix for Kids and Games DVD which were something lacking in 95% of the Linux Distributions.

If you do not use any other Linux distributions this is the one one should always have.

I cannot find anything wrong with this distribution when I format my hard disk once a year towards December, it is the first one that goes into the hard disk as the flag bearer of Linux and other distributions are installed afterward.

5. Poseidon Linux

Poseidon with 2390 points comes fifth.

Poseidon Linux not Scientific Linux (actually this name is misleading and does not have any scientific packages in this distribution) takes a big spot in my scale by a wide margin for packaging productive utilities for scientific (including statistics) and business purposes and for schools.

Its score of 2390 which was very close to PCLinux but had more packages than PCLinux.

They are inkscape, blender, statistics and plotting packages but it is on the heavyweight category and downloading is slow mainly due to not having a torrent facility.

But it has CD version too and again it is a Debian/Ubuntu derivative.

In spite of its FATTY layer I like it very much and one has almost everything one needs in one shoe.

6. Pinguy/Pinguy Eee

Pinguy/Pinguy Eee comes sixth with 2385.

For the time being Pinguy and Pinguy Eee are the best innovative Ubuntu derivative which is in the market and the score is 2385 which is very close to the Gold Standard and well above Unity.

Out of the Ubuntu derivatives this is the most eye catching feature filled derivative to entice Linux newbies as well as savvy guys / girls.

It has Cloud Utilities, Light Scribe and it almost look like apple Mac for one who has never seen a Apple Mac.

I have the feeling Ubuntu's Unity has taken a leaf out of Pinguy and Pinguy Eee for netbooks and laptops.

Its grub file could not figure out my other distributions and that was why it was not in my box up till now.

The new version has now ironed out this minor glitch and I have installed it with 5 other distributions in my laptop which I upgraded to 500 GiB recently.

Interestingly enough, this is the one I boot first since I am getting attached to it day by day.

It now does a good job with GRUB and recognizes all the other Linux derivatives.

It will certainly take the tablets not by surprise but by its own imagination.

7. Dynabolic

Dynabolic comes seventh with 2290.

Dynabolic 3.0.0 beta is currently available at www.linuxtracker.com.org torrent and this was one of the oldest Linux music distributions. It was created by Denis Rogo an Italian musician. It was in hibernation (version 2) but lately has created the version 3 for download.

I call him the Bob Marley of computer music.

It is feature packed but cannot be installed as yet.

It scores thumping 2290 points was not a surprise for me.

8. PCLinux

PCLinux comes 8th with 2255.

My favorite distribution gets 2255 points which is well below the 2500 points which I have allocated for the Hypothetical Gold Standard but a future candidate for that award.

It has promised to introduce bit 64 version.

The tested version for this study was in 32 bits.

64 bits version is currently available.

Even though, it has no special features it sticks to Linux base with administrative functions and very stable once properly configured.

It gets lot of points for it's web site and the digital magazine which it maintains.

The package management is excellent and lets you install all the packages easily from the repository. To be on record this is the only distribution which has a usable Skype (except perhaps Linvo). It also does not bother one with updates unlike Suse. It is a KDE desktop and has two Mini versions, one LXDE and the standard KDE. Once installed there is very little maintenance if firewall is correctly configured and easy with downloads and remove redundant files at boot time and if it is run on 24/7 schedule it does a good cron job too.

No wonder it was my favorite and may be so for others too.

Ubuntu's departure from traditional base would be another reason.

It is bit slow at boot time and K-torrent is good (it may be bit slow because of my heavy daily work and downloads) and if one is using it for light work, one may not find the slow boot up a problem. Even one who is a light user of the computer it is a good practice for the distribution to run 24 hours at least once a week for maintenance which it does automatically well past midnight.

My reason for choosing it.

It is very stable and stands 8th in the ranks.

9. Puppy

Puppy comes 9th with 1910.

It is Small and Beautiful size ~100MB!

It is Live booting from CD and USB flash drive.

It runs from RAM, making it unusually fast even in old PCs and in netbooks with solid state storage media.

It Includes a wide range of applications: word processors, spreadsheets, Internet browsers, games, image editors and many other useful utilities.

Puppy is easy to use and little technical knowledge is assumed. Most hardware is automatically detected.

Who is the founder?

Barry Kauler from Australia.

10. Simply Mepis

AntiX

Simply Mepis with AntiX ranks 10th.

Simply Mepis is high in my honour's list with its stable KDE desktop, K3B, the CD/DVD burning utility with a cleaning utility called sweeper included to delete redundant files.

It also has AntiX for older computers. Taylor Swift which has taken roots from AntiX is still not yet mature enough to be recommended as a general purpose distribution but AntiX is light weight and robust. Mepis does an overall good job of covering new and old computers which is somewhat mandatory now with lot of changes happening in the IT market and some proprietary Operating Systems abandoning their customer base and luring them to go for newer versions without substantial benefits for the average user except the eye catching cosmetic changes and that also at the expense of overheads which include battery usage and additional expenses for the RAM etc.

Newer version has LibreOffice and all the utilities one needs in a CD or DVD which is less than 1 GiB and save the time of download.

It scores 1880 in my scoring scale which is value for money.

It ranks 10th in my ranking scale.

11. Dream Studio

Ubuntu Dream Studio comes 11th with 1775 points.

Ubuntu's Unity-Dream Studio!

Is it a dream come true for newbies?

I think so and thumbs up for this distribution which I could download overnight with 2.1 GiB.

There were only four seeders but it was pretty fast. Go and download it and increase the number of seeders in proportion to leechers and enjoy the Unity experience.

It is a new experience for old hand of Linux like me who never used Ubuntu on regular basis except for demonstrations.

Regular Ubuntu users will grumble but I will tell you what to do. Go ahead and have both old version and new version in the same box and enjoy the difference.

Sinhala capability was there which I did not test but probably needs some ironing out which is another plus point.

It has LibreOffice and Blender a new version (Maya replacement).

Please do not call it Apple like but call it;

"This is Unity Linux Desktop".

Sure it is a winner at the time of debt and cash crisis.

For good effects find a good compatible graphic card. That may be the only thing one may have to change in one's computer. My old computer's graphic card was not enough to take advantage of Unity.

The few glitches I had with the Unity CD with workplaces has been reasonably taken care of and I could load all the workplaces with a program running within and with a mouse click it goes into full screen image.

Play with it and enjoy the experience.

I do not know how far one can configure it to one's own needs but it is good as it is why configure and make a mess out of it?

It score is 1775.

Rest with points scored.

11. Dream Studio Ubuntu	1755
12. Trisquel	1660
13. Suse	1560
14. Sabayon	1430
15. Swift Linux	1415
16. Ubuntu-Unity	1405
17. PureOs	1385
18. Salix	1380

19. Kubuntu	1355
20. Fedora	1325
21. Berry	1275
22. Linux Mint	1260
23. CloudUSB	1240
24. Apodio	1165
25. Vinux	1130

Incognito comes 26th and it is for anonymous web browsing and cannot be installed.

I have missed ArtistX which would score around 2600 and could be in place of Ultimate Linux (If you do not like games Linux DVD). It is also an Ubuntu/Debian derivative and for Audio/Video and artistic work.

I can report to you now it got 2610 points, just 10 points less than Ultimate Linux. The difference is only marginal, one is for gamers and the other for artists.

GnuArtist got 2445 points, less points scored, indeed due to not incorporating proprietary software and keeping itself to Gnome base.

Other versions not included was the result of inability to download or incompatibility with my old graphic cards.

Chapter 17

Naming the Linux Distributions (Categories)

My Way

Now that I have finished scoring cross section of the Linux Distributions, to render and make my future classification easy, I have decided to change from the Weight Category based on Apes Family, (simply to spare the abuse of this Family especially the common monkeys-who venture into the city looking for food and poisoned by some citizens) and used an alternative method based on the distribution's functionality.

This will certainly create lot of flames (now that the war is over I do not mind the urban flames not forest fire) but I got to get on with my naming strategy.

1. NuKe Variety.

I wanted to name it nude but NuKe is OK since most of us in this country pronounce NuKE as Nude anyway.

These are bare bone distributions almost stripped of all the attire but the skin is beautiful as in fish and birds, the nakedness (or the NuKe) is barely visible.

The core utilities based on Slackware is the PROTOTYPE.

They do not have X-Windows

Unity

Arch

Gentoo.

These are for the developers and developers are generally invincible.

2. BiKi (Ni) Category

Second category is BiKi(Ni) and only clad and covered in G-string sized X-windows.

4MLinux

TinyCore

CoreLinux

Slitaz

They fit in a Mini CDs.

These are for the old school type of Linux users not worried about what others do, inherently lazy and nobody knows they do exist.

They are in the minority.

3. LyKe Category

LyKe, another typical Sri-Lankan wrong pronunciation.

Like NuKe it sounds Linux.

The name comes from the LyKa, the dog that was sacrificed in space by Russian.

These distributions are one's close friend like a dog and a work slave.

These are the workhorse type of of distributions and naming any one of them as a PROTOTYPE is gross injustice to ones not mentioned.

Majority of the Linux distributions fall into this category.

These remain active as long as there are followers in the community and sometimes suddenly disappear after a stint.

4. Carnival Category

Fourth is the carnival type dressed in Ragtags (Ragtag Variety), as seen in Brazilian street carnival from almost nothing to exotic.

Puppy

PCLinuxFullmonty

Knoppix

Ultimate Linux

Artistix

Uberstudent

Poseidon

Apodio

Musix

LiveLinuxGamers and many more fall into this group.

They are very special that is why they dress differently in street or bazaar carnivals.

They are generally task based like games, arts or science.

5. King Con Category

Fifth, I call the King Con (con as in a lie) Type, almost non-existent in the Linux Community but when the King or the President of a country incarcerate a developer in a palace or presidential house requesting them for top security for the palace and their kith and kin to hide all the unpleasant details.

But in actual fact it is something like SliTaz and lot of Cookies added as long as the developer/s is/are incarcerated and deprived from his normal developmental activity.

All kings thinks bigger is always better and their is no other thinking in them.

LPS that comes from DOD is one of them which can be loaded with security piping that no information either gets in or gets out.

This is a nightmare distribution for true Linux developers.

Chapter 18

When One is troubled with Windows What one can do?

It is strange that when one is troubled with Windows he or she goes into shell and blame oneself and not the operating system.

It is the opposite when one is troubled with Linux.

If he / she is a one who comes from the Windows background without batting an eyelid he / she blames the distribution as if the whole hell has descended on him / her.

It is often a minor glitch he or she has overlooked to configure or may be downloading a suitable alternative package or worse come file a bug report to which a ready solution is available within 6 weeks. If that does not help one can swap the distribution and select one that suits and download it.

One problem with this approach is if one is not using a torrent download (even this can be painful if there is one seeder who has gone into hibernation at night-simply switched off the computer) it can be time consuming. The download time can be awfully long and be painful (I have enough of stories often due to failure of the Telecoms but now, never or do not complain because I download several at a time and I know one will be finished by morning when I am in deep sleep and dreaming some bizarre episode of Cloud Computing like star wars of yesteryear).

But once one has a CD (ideally D.V.D with almost everything one needs in one pack) the live session is breezy and installation is cakewalk if not catwalk.

Only thing Linux guys forget is to keep it running 24 hours (cron jobs at midnight are vital to get rid of the junk files that collect when one switches off the computer) and leave seeds for others to access at least once or twice a week.

If you are lazy use a the sweeper or do it manually which I prefer now because of the frequent downloads.

Now come to Window guys/girls.

Steps

1. Do not blame yourself.

2. It is often the operating system at fault.

3. It can be due to a corrupt file or large macro sitting on the file and spying on you.

4. The pet devise to blame is the latest virus and I bet you you will not have a solution this side of 6 months.

With so many holes in the operating system which Microsoft will never able plug and then they will promise you the new version is very beautiful (but very slow to run unless you doubled up your RAM) and one should change and upgrade and it works better (of course till the next ultra new version is ready for upgrade).

You are in this vicious cycle (V.C) and never get out of it.

If a guy of my age descends on me with a problem, I do not try to convert the guy to Linux fearing one gets a heart attack.

I ask a few questions.

If it it a pirated copy.

If the answer is yes, thrash the pirated copy and get a copyrighted version.

This is I am openly campaigning for the guy to remain with Microsoft. Microsoft should be happy with my efforts now but I do not charge anything for this advice.

The poor guy has to pay through his nose anyway.

Do not forget the virus guard and that also will cost you some quids.

Get somebody to format and install, I won't do that for you unless he or wishes to have a Linux distribution dual booted.

He has to spend a half a day with me with food and beverages ready and ample.

This is Christmas time anyway.

If the guy got no money, then the scenario changes.

I ask what are the things that he uses computer for, regularly. Invariably, the answer is that he uses the email and nothing else to be in contact with the family and friends.

Then I give him a breezy Live CD and ask the guy to use it till he himself try to find a remedy for the malady or ultimately ditch Microsoft and ask me to install the new distribution in his computer. The last outcome of course works well for Linux and I of course have to have two visits instead of one.

That of course keeps our friendship lasting and viable.

Who says Microsoft is bad.

It makes "my sphere of activity" to enlarge and expand.

Chapter 19

Linux Distribution for Netbooks

I have some bad news for netbook users.

If you are a Linux user, the community has left you high and dry.

Thankfully only two distributions that came out three years ago and Netrunner Linux would support the netbooks.

I will dispense with Netrunner 4.2.1 which I downloaded first.

It is pretty good if you have enough RAM.

It comes in both 32 bits and 64 bits versions and I recommend it without any hesitation for laptops but for netbooks, make sure you have enough RAM.

It takes up over 8 GiB and hence cannot be mounted on a Flash drive below 8 GiB and I hope the developers would trim it down to suit for Flash Drive / Pendrive use below 4 GiB.

But my top recommendation is Pingue Eee which does a good job of being relatively recent and having all the software.

Eeebunbtu would boot up your Netbook but has only limited software range.

Hurry up and download Pingue Eee, my favorite and report to its home base if you have any problems.

The rest of the distributions I tested except CloudUSB is not worth any mention here.

Cloud USB is Ubuntu 10 derivative and the developers have got into a frozen state due to Ubuntu's Unity project which left all Ubuntu users having a netbook high and dry.

Sometime ago, I suggested the developers of CloudUSB have a fresh look at its future development and they could take a leaf out of NetRunner 4.2.1 and think afresh.

Remember Ubuntu/Canonical does not support Kubuntu now and they are doing a great job and Netrunner is a Kubuntu derivative.

Ubuntu 12.04.1, (LTS-Long Term Support), SuSe 12.2, PCLINux and most of the standard distributions do not support netbooks and one has to remember Linux took off and its resurgence was due to netbooks and abandoning its netbook base is not a good ploy and has left a bad taste with (newbies) Linux users.

This is why Linux is lately becoming less and less popular due to new Desktop Development (not utility) craze (I call it D.D.C for short).

Update on Linux on Netbooks

This little writing would not have come if not for our industrial action.

First of all, I must thank my young colleagues for initiating and prolonging the action for the third month without a break.

I must thank my bank manager for extending a loan to buy the netbook with SuSe Enterprise 10 on it.

Mind you we are without a salary for 3 months.

I would not have found this netbook lying in a corner, if not for the strike.

Everyday, I come out looking for a new adventure and window (mind you not Windows) shopping and getting involved in a long conversation (used to be very brief when we were working) with anybody who is somebody in the town.

It was a welcome change.

The extra time was utilized to find the appropriate Linux distribution/s for the new netbook.

What you need apart from the netbook and money are as following

1. Gparted, an old version (new one might not boot in a netbook).

2. Pinguy Eee (It is actually a PIN GUY in Sinhala-Pinata Pahalaunu Man/Bloke)

3. Easy Peasy-2009-Ubuntu derivative

4.Puppeee a Puppy Linux derivative especially for netbooks

5. Couple of 8 GiB Flash Drives

6. Couple of Mini DVDs and a USB DVD Writer.

7. Ideally on strike and sleep well on day time.

8. Do all this when everybody is sleeping and Internet is not very busy.

Steps

UnetBootIn

1. Boot up and erase the hard disk with Suse for good with Gparted and prepare the hard disk the way I liked.

2. Install Pingue Eee with a relatively large home partition to place the images of the distributions mentioned above, if one is downloading them. I had all of them in my my CD/DVD collection downloaded over the last three years (for testing) with images as well as Live DVDs.

One needs the images or convert it/them to image/s using K3B, if UnetBootIn is used for preparing Live USB.

Pingue 11.04 has Live USB/CD-DVD Creator instead of UnetBootIn.

3. Download NetRunner 4.2.1 and copy the image to Download folder.

4. In my case I copied it to a DVD

5. Boot Up Pingue Eee with 8 GiB Flash Drive attached.

6. Open the UnetBootIn

7. Give the path to the NetRunner Image or the Easy Peasy Image.

8. Click OK and go and make a cup of good coffee if you are an impatient guy / girl.

9. Before you can finish the coffee the Flash Drive will be ready for booting.

10. Why did I select the latest NetRunner?

It has GIMP the latest 2.8 version which is pretty good.

Depending on your liking the other distributions can also be run live or on a Flash Drive which I have done and they all work OK.

But take care with Puppy Linux since one is not able to reverse any action committed by you except reinstalling the distribution one has downloaded.

I have tried Joli OS, Cloud USB and PCLinux 2010 and all of them worked OK.

All new versions of Ubuntu, Suse, PCLinux and Knoppix do not boot and have left you with no choices.

They have become hunky dory!

However I copied Knoppix 7.0.4 CD to a download folder and prepared a Live Flash Drive to boot with my other computers.

It looks like images over 1 GiB cannot be copied to a netbook but downloading an image (large) by torrent may be a way round that problem if one has a fast Internet connection.

If you are pressed for time, form a trade union and go on strike for at least 3 months and all your creativity will be recharged in no time.

Good luck with your free time on Linux freedom.

One can boot Linux from a MicroSD card but I use them for loading photos from my digital camera / or from the phone.

Linux Multi System USB booting CD

If you have nothing else to do, I have got some work for you.

1. Just buy a few USB sticks or a large sized one or two USB sticks.

2. Download your favorite Linux images, any number of your choices.

3. Download Linux MultiSystem CD image and write it on a CD, by torrent.

4. Boot it up Live and launch the MultiSystem Utility.

5. Stick a USB stick to one of the ports in your system.

6. Run the program and install any number of Linux distribution to be booted to the USB stick (that would depend on the sizes of the distributions and the capacity of your USB stick.)

7. Restart the computer, remove the CD and run the distribution from the Flash Drive (the USB stick).

Up till now this program could be obtained (installed) from Pendrive Linux site and could be run on Ubuntu or an Ubuntu derivative.

Not on Debian and Debian has a different utility.

Guess what one can do?

I installed MultiSystem distribution on the USB stick to begin with and three other distributions that can boot Netbooks, including Puppy. This is handy since Netbooks do not have CD/DVD drives.

I installed Multisystem utility on the Peppermint Linux that was installed on my Netbook.

Repeated the above procedures on a Standard SD card instead of on a Flash Drive.

I stick it in to an appropriate port, and it is there ready to RUN on RAM in an emergency.

I included few Rescue distributions in the lot.

I must say, I had few hiccups!

Suse Linux and Fedora Linux do not cohabit well with other distributions (they are not Ubuntu based). There is no problem, if one is using only one distribution in the USB stick, but its defeats the MultiSystem very intentions (i.e have multiple operating systems in one place).

Having as many distributions as one may wish.

NetBootiIn and YUMI do not perform, as well as the MutiSystem Utility. It is number one for me but it is Ubuntu based and not Universal for all the Linux distributions, as at present.

Having it on a Live CD is the simple solution MultiSystem developers have opted for.

Teething Problems with Multi-System

Here is an update on Muti-System USB Boot utility not YUMI which is basically windows utility.

Pendrive Linux site gives graphic descriptions of all the utilities.

It is the best available SITE.

But the Linux Magazine described a Linux Live CD.

Its name ms_its_precision_r9.iso.

After lot of digital digging, I found it at Linux Software foundation and downloaded it (which is 700 MB).

It is a French creation and one needs to press F2 (boots very fast) to get the English (if you are not French).

It has an Ubuntu Desktop and has Multi System Utility to prepare USB Multi-booting.

My advise is for you to download the favorite distributions ISOs to your download folder and then use the Muti System Utility. I used my Peppermint Linux, in root (cannot use it as an ordinary user) and tried to boot ms_its_precision_r9.iso distribution.

I tried it twice and GRUB Menu directed me to MultiSystem in French and English but its squash (Live file system) file is not properly extracted into the USB or faulty and is not loaded with initrm.

This is probably due to dropping some of the files that are used by Ubuntu in Live Mode.

Chapter 20

Linux Distribution Update

Very Subjective

Nobody should get offensive of this post.

I have deliberately excluded Teeny Weeny Linux that are in my book except Puppy Linux.

This is the consumer world and I have my own choices to make when on strike or on holiday mood.

Strike is also a demonstrable, democratic, consumer activity which politicians do not see that way.

They have instead a Commonwealth Conferences to beg for AIDS, the Disease.

Education is a Common Wealth in this Country, not Private Property!

The views expressed are very subjective and won't have any bearing to statistics of current Linux usage.

In fact, I am more concerned about why Linux penetration is not active as it used to be than its user activity.

I am getting used to the rut due to the procrastinated and prolong strike or the general use of the term, the industrial action.

Yes it is very difficult to penetrate a good idea like Linux to ordinary masses.

It is also difficult to penetrate an idea the Education is a Common Wealth of our people (If one is not using it prudently, that is his or her onus or responsibility) or the name sake free education we enjoyed and want to foster in this century too.

It is very difficult to deal with politician with dud brains, just like it was very difficult for me to try to introduce various Linux distributions for general use in our school system and classrooms.

Yes, there is Hanthana Linux, a derivative of Fedora is out there but it is very difficult to get a copy or download in this blessed country in which we pay through our noses for the services for which we pay dearly and get only 10% output or throughput, the productivity which is less than 10%.

We had been boasting about war victory for last three years but the productivity has hit rock bottom except for few privileged personalities with political connections.

In the University for the first time the productivity almost hitting the Zero rating.

That Zero rating made me to venture into many uncharted territories but relatively minimal political involvement but my political statements at the time of Commonwealth Conference is loud and clear.

Politician cannot produce productivity but only we can do it for them but they have to tore the line with the global trends.

We cannot reinvent the wheel.

Productivity comes with only good pay.

If you pay pittance the returns is a pittance.

Let me come to Linux, I was reading the Linux Magazine today but there I always read the editors page before even glancing on the free distribution and this time it happened to be Mageia.

He was commenting on the news item that Google is paying 50% of the salary for 10 years to the dependent, if an employee is deceased.

WOW but his comments on this deal, an intellectual exercise by itself which I won't repeat here.

A lesser politician cannot understand his logic but go buy the Magazine and read it for yourself, it is his intellectual property.

Now to my list in order of my preference.

1. Puppy Linux for its minimal use of resources and awesome collection of utilities including cloud compatibility.

There are many derivatives, for Games, Cloud, Netbooks, Laptops and Desktops.

It is easy on you and can carry in a Pendrive.

2. Pinguy Linux is the only one which has a current derivative for old (netbooks) and new computers.

It is very pleasing experience.

3. Ubuntu for its bold steps, moving with the trends and cloud capability.

4. Ultimate Linux/Tango / Studio and now Kiwi and Super OS. The last two integrate classic genome with Unity.

This is what I said when Ubuntu was contemplating on Unity (provide Unity and Gnome in one distribution and everybody will be happy).

So Ubuntu derivatives will do what Canonical won't do!

Canonical has abandoned Kubuntu and NetRunner is a good hit with netbooks.

This is a good lesson to Fedora and Mandrake and Mageia.

5. Five has to be Arch Linux for its vision and dedication to produce a minimalistic Quality Product without fringes.

They are command line experts but why work only on black and white. Introducing a minimalistic desktop to play few games (4M Linux tradition) will make its global penetration cakewalk and in no time, when one is fed up with the black terminal, who would not play a few games, at least DOS games?

Light desktop like Deli Linux will make a huge impact globally and will make it climb up in popularity almost like Puppy Linux.

Having said that Bridge Linux, Manjaro, Archbang and Criunchbang (Debian derivative) have done the honors for Arch Linux.

6. Number six is Debian for its enormous resources, one will never be able to tap in a lifetime.

7. Sabayon comes seventh and it is Gentoo based and beautiful with many desktop versions including KDE and Gnome

8. Knoppix has come down below Debian simply because I had to download it for the third time. The graphic installer for demonstration purposes to Linux newbies is still not working to my satisfaction.

I am sure by Christmas time Knoppix will climb up to 3rd if not fourth place.

The current Knoppix 7.5 has ironed out all the problems and is my favorite now.

9. PCLinux and it is lacking in innovation even though the KDE is solid.

10. Korarra Linux Fedora derivative and not Fedora 17.

11. Even though, Suse has not kept its place in the top 10, it is beautiful but heavy and lack simple utilities.

12. Linus Mint, has dropped in my list and unfortunately it is in its 13th edition.

It is trying to do too many things in one go.

Ubuntu is focused on its Vision for the Future but Linux Mint is not.

It is playing an open market game which is a spoiler for me.

It is not a game-changer at all.

13. Mandriva / Mageia / Rosa and I wish them good luck and they should follow Knoppix, Kiwi and Super Os examples to get back on track.

It is humanly possible but Russians are not creative nowadays unlike in the nineteen sixties when cold war was in full swing.

I did not want to have 13th but decided to include Mageia since the copy I got with the Linux Magazine did not boot up with my old IBM which I have hacked with various new additions.

It does not have auto-detect utility for hard disks.

I won't recommend it for general use yet.

They say number 13 is unlucky, may be so for Mandriva and Mageia.

There won't be 14th in my list it is for you to decide the next in the list.

I must tell you why I use Linux.

Number one is FUN now.

It used to be SECURITY when I started it.

I have used my Main Linux Box for over 10 years, day in and day out (more because of the strike action) but I never had to make any changes after the Firewall was configured properly.

Worst scenario was that I forgot the password (I haven't had any need for one year and I simply forgot it but no harm done yet) for root and the user briefly.

That was unintended disaster!

I was up all night and doing sorting out of all my Linux distributions for installing on my laptop, three months in advance of the December recess from academic activities (again due to strike action and no creative work to do). and I could not start the computer after restart having tested a Puppy Linux derivative.

Absentminded prof!

I have now decided to write all my passwords in a book including my email passwords.

I also forgot the email password and Ubuntu One password too in a momentary loss of my intellectual capacity due to (no sleep at all) no valid reason just gone blank (not a stroke) and I was working nonstop on a Sunday from 2 p.m till Monday morning, knowing very well, I do not have to worry about work on Monday.

Mind you Sunday is my Sleep Day.

So if you are on a Holiday or on industrial action, take care of your intellectual capabilities and passwords.

That is called disuse atrophy in medicine, in my case it was the brain.

It is time for my brain to drain, possibly abroad.

I recovered from this ordeal in a matter of one hour without sleeping or having a break and that was another achievement during this prolong industrial action.

The usual remedy, in my case, not to panic, but go to sleep and wake up rejuvenated.

All lost memories are back in a flash.

Last time when I forgot the email password I had to toil for solid three months to get back to base, nearly a decade ago.

It was horrible experience and I instituted a protocol that ran good stead for me (mainly due to mental apathy and lack of sleep this time round).

All these due to lethargy and industrial action and disuse atrophy. Strike is not a good recipe for intellectuals and only good for political purposes.

Our strike has taken a political trend and a turn unfortunately.

God blessing we have a Commonwealth Conference now.

Hope it will be an eyeopener!

Chapter 21

Booting Netbook with a SD Card

I was lucky to find a netbook with reasonable RAM with hard disk more than 100 GiB.

It also had SuSe enterprise edition to make a good buy in Sri-Lanka.

There was no buyer for it until I discovered it in a shop in Kandy.

Dealer was not a computer expert but a good salesman.

I could negotiate a good price having convinced him nobody will buy it (except perhaps me) with Linux as an operating system and if he has to install Microsoft there will be additional cost for him.

He won't be able to boot it from a Flashdrive and he needs a USB DVD ROM to boot Microsoft.

That was some additional expense for the buyer.

Then I came home since I did not have spare cash (they stopped the salary for 3 months) because of the strike action.

Three months was a long time and I negotiated a loan from the bank and bought it, a week after initial negotiation.

Having bought it I left it without using it since Suse 10 was very old for me with OpenOffice instead of Libre Office.

In addition, I could not get any additional software without registering with Novel (just like one register with Microsoft).

This was annoying for me to say the least.

I did not won't a somewhat Virtual Guy taking control of my Linux Freedom.

Equally, I did not want to lose warranty.

Then I realized only a few of the Linux distribution were compatible with netbooks.

Finally, I found Pinguy with all the software (11 series of Pinguy-Ubuntu derivative) including gParted and UnetBootIn and even Ubuntu One.

So one day I eased everything and booted and installed Pinguy.

I of course tried resizing the partition to get some space for Pinguy leaving behind Suse intact, but it did not boot Suse after resizing.

In any case the partitioning done by the foreign vendor was horrible and did not have any understanding of Linux I believe.

That is the long story and the little story is how I booted it with a SDHC Memory Card.

Again I had to delay this due to monetary reason.

Two days after we suspended the strike action I was in full swing and saw a 16 GiB SDHC Card and bought it using my credit card.

Methods and Materials.

1. Netbook

2. Linux image written on a DVD (Pinguy in this case).

3. Couple of Flashdrives.

4. USB Hard drive.

5. SD or SDHC

6. DVD RW Writer, optional.

7. Laptop for getting things ready with a DVD.

8. If not a Desktop.

In my case the downloading was done with the desktop and all the Linux images were copied subsequently to the USB Hard disk.

Steps

1. Install Pinguy.

2. Using Pinguy prepare either USB Flash Drive (UnietBootIn) or USB hard drive as spare Live systems (Using Live DVD).

3. Boot Pinguy with SDHC card in slot.

4. Use gParted to partition SDHC Card.

5. First partition has to be FAT32 (in my case 4 GB FAT 32, 4 GiB NTFS and 8 GiB Ext4)

6. Run UnetBootIn and I gave the path to where my Linux Pinguy image was (in the USB Hard Disk). Be careful of the nomenclature of the disk names (HDD 1 Sda2, Sda 3 etc) and where it should be installed (in this case SDHC Card).

In a few minutes one has a bootable SD Card.

7. Boot it to see whether the installation is right.

8. Follow the same procedure for Flashdrives and test to see whether they work and remove them and place them in a safe place (Use them in case your original system breaks down. It rarely happens with Linux though and in my case never but when accidentally I format a partition with an operating system installed, I fall, back to the live CD/DVD.

Now it is Flashdrives and SD Cards both of which are environmentally sound as compared to CD/DVDs which are not.

Good luck if you are trying my experiments to get a hang of Linux.

Chapter 22

Update

When I thought of writing this I wanted to give plus or minus points for some of the lapses in development that has come onto surface or in existence. In other words whether they deviated from my original analysis in 2010 and become better or worse.

On second thoughts, I thought it not the way round.

The point scheme was designed having seen the proliferation of Linux distributions and some with major lapses.

For example fault in the Grub file was was one.

Not having a Live CD/DVD was another.

Third was not having a home page or ability make constructive criticism.

All these lapses they have been patched up and most of the distributions that I tested were implementing, all the basic functionality for general use.

Why bother awarding points for a second time?

In any case, my point system was biased towards usability and not for technical achievements.

My only grouse now is based on the fact that most of the distributions not having 32 bit versions or Physical Address Extension (PAE) for old hardware.

For example PCLinux which was only in 32 bit but had PAE when Texstar was heading the team. But when he took a back seat the next generation went straight ahead and changed to 64 bit version.

The 32 bit they put out did not have full coverage for the old hardware and graphic cards.

I have lost number of graphic cards and RAM cards when I was using only Windows. Only once, I remember losing a RAM card was with Suse, my favorite then. This was due to bloating (It was a FAT distribution) of the KDE desktop with only 1 GiB RAM in my old computer.

I never lost a graphic card while using Linux for the last 15 years. Most of the Linux distributions, if they cannot configure or detect the graphic card at boot time warn you, in a live session (kernel panic) and won't go beyond and try booting.

But the new PCLinux that came after Texstar FROZE my computer and at the end it burned the graphic card, making it unusable.

I was so annoyed, I could not find another replacement.

The developers were bloating the operating system without adding functionality.

In actual fact it slows the computer.

Instead of upgrading the RAM I changed the operating system which was less demanding on my old system.

Suffice is to say I never used PCLinux on my old computer and switched to Peppermint which is light on my old hardware and working fine and it is my workhorse (Peppermint 4) now.

The Peppermint has moved to version (6) six and I did not upgrade (which was my usual practice) my system.

I usually reinstall the new version without formatting the home partition. Then I have to add my favorite software which takes at least two days.

That to me is a big strain (with slow download speed of our Telecoms).

I have a cardinal rule.

If the system works for you fine do not change with the next hype in the developer world.

The best use of this book is for you to choose, the Linux system that works best for your hardware and drop the others.

If a particular distribution is lacking something, what I do is dual boot it with another Linux system that has the utility.

In any case my computer has minimum of four Linux distributions installed.

If you are dual booting with Windows it has to go first and the Linux second. Windows have this funny habit of ignoring Linux.

It is an intractable IT disease.

I said, I won't talk about system requirement and hardware but that basic knowledge is mandatory if you need to keep your hardware doing donkey work for years.

As I said earlier, I have dismantled 9 out of 10 computers I used to cut down on my electricity bill. The computer I am using now is about to bust with the SATA hard disk giving problem.

I did not buy (not available even second hand) another SATA but bought a new 1 terrabyte laptop hard disk and stored my data, mostly isos in it.Thus regular emptying of my home partition was all that was necessary to prolong the half life of the hardware.

If it packs (hard disk) up due to any reason, I have a Linux distribution installed in the USB hard drive.

I do not have to wait, I am up and running again after big fall.

It is just common sense in computing.

RAM, Memory and Graphic Cards

In computer architecture, shared graphics memory refers to a design where the graphics chip does not have its own dedicated memory, and instead shares the main system RAM with the CPU and other components.

This design is used with many integrated graphics solutions to reduce the cost and complexity of the motherboard design, as no additional memory chips are required on the board. There is usually some mechanism (via the BIOS or a jumper setting) to select the amount of system memory to use for graphics, which means that the graphics system can be tailored to only use as much RAM as is actually required, leaving the rest free for applications.

A side effect of this is that when some RAM is allocated for graphics, it becomes effectively unavailable for anything else, for an example computer with 512 MiB RAM set up with 64MiB graphics RAM will appear to the operating system and user to only have 48 MiB RAM installed.

The disadvantage of this design is lower performance because system RAM usually runs slower than dedicated graphics RAM, and there is more contention as the memory bus has to be shared with the rest of the system.

It may also cause performance issues with the rest of the system if it is not designed with the fact in mind that some RAM will be 'taken away' by graphics.

Gamers please take a note of the above hardware issues.

I still use 1 GiB of memory.

I have a stock of RAM from the dismantled computers.

Another subtle point is, do not fiddle with hardware components, if the system is running.

The computer builds a static electric field around it when running. One has to use gloves which are anti-static, if not the computer may fail to start with the next change of components.

It is not like changing oil in a motor vehicle.

The computer is built to run 24/7 schedule, if you do not why use or have one?

Go to a public library and save cost for you and the country.

Chapter 23

Wisdom Browser-Browser Hater

I am beginning to become a Browser Hater.

Most of the browser are good at eavesdropping at best but worse at preventing cookies with commercial advertisement.

I am glad that I use live CDs, light weight Linux distributions and light weight non-intrusive browsers most of the time.

This is not true for many guys and girls using the Internet.

I thought, if I develop a browser these are the qualities, I will focus.

1. W for Wise Browser who is not eavesdropping on your habits.

2. I for individual freedom and the protection of the individual from all the vulnerabilities of the Internet specially KIDS.

3. S for Simple. It should be simple to use even to a KID.

4. D for dependability on all circumstances and should not feed the information to DOD or the State.

5. O for obliging, objective and obedience to the cause.

6. M for minimalism on resources of one's computer and it should be light weight.

None of the commercial browsers fall into WISDOM category and a few Linux come close to the qualities mentioned above.

With cloud computing in mind Amazon has developed a light weight browser called Silk to use with the Kindle Fire but it seems that Amazon cannot keep up with the promise.

I have some more points especially with kids in mind.

If one types play and game on a browser the search engine with a few clicks will invariable detoured to a pornographic site to lure kids and young ones.

That is how it operates now.

I have few suggestions for a future browser development which parents can use at home and teachers at school.

I think only Linux can address this and commercial browsers will never go to that extend.

1. The browser should be linked to a alight weight distribution like Bodhi or Arch (Manjaro).

2. It should have a cloud access (a password and an email address to access) through a lightweight browser for the front end.

3. The back end browser should have protocols and priorities.

The user should have the sole access (in this case parent or teacher) of the contents in the private cloud.

The service provider should have a maintenance password of it own but no full access.

In making the children passwords the degree of difficulty in access should depend, on the age of the child and the parent / teacher should be able to monitor it and the content should be appropriate for the stage of development of the child.

That part of the cloud can be made private with all the public clouds reserved for the grown ups.

All this can be achieved with meticulous planning.

The cloud can be used to streamline content and protect our children worldwide.

4. There should be a language element for rare languages and search engines should be developed tailored for these languages and they should be used to bypass major languages.

Otherwise few languages will dominate the web and language like Pali (original Buddhism was handed down by Pali) will become extinct which is a shame.

5. The front end browser should be able to access the particular server end browser in that particular language.

By this method we might be able to preserve these languages in pristine form for posterity.

There are lot of missing points and I hope developers will look at this scenario and teachers would provide inputs as the progress in development takes it course.

Why I hate Nosy, Bulky Browsers?

I will list them first for easy reading and relate an incident that happened.

1. They are FAT.

2. The have what are called cookies. These cookies are very oily full of Cholesterol.

3. They are Lazy as a result of eating FAT Cookies.

4. All of these I can excuse.

To be fat is no crime. To be Lazy is a Sri-Lankan pastime and I can excuse that too.

5. But I cannot tolerate FAT person being nosy.

All these browsers are Nosy.

In fact, like FBI and KGB they are paranoid and watch every move you make out there in the web.

There is nothing called privacy.

6. You may say I have a password when I read my mail.

It is just a joke.

Your password is remembered for posterity.

You might or yeah, it saves me typing a cryptic password.

But if the search engine remembers it how can it be a password?

Coming from Linux background this is violation number one.

Who gives permission to the browser.

Nobody but like a school principal the browser assumes the authority.

7. Some cookies do eavesdropping for advertisers especially porn.

8. Where does one end up with?

Your boss is angry with you.

Try to find an excuse to sack you.

You inadvertently forget to log off and close the browser and pretend to be doing some mundane work.

He excuses for a minute and sits in.

Goes through the history.

Copy the history and sends an email to himself with a date tag.

He does this for a month or so and asks you for an interview. Some paranoid bosses may have even surreptitiously opened your email (DID NOT LOG OFF BUT ONLY CLOSED THE BROWSER) and BROWSE YOUR PRIVATE MAIL TOO.

You have no defense and fired.

Whom to blame not your boss but the BIG FAT BROWSER?

What is the end result.

Your boss is paranoid and you too are paranoid and the productivity comes down drastically.

9. Same scenario can be in your home unless you have a little network like what I have at home.

Everyone has a computer terminal (Linux not Microsoft) and the guests also has a terminal for an emergency.

Even if one does not have anything to hide like a simple Buddhist monk every individual deserve some space of privacy.

Breaking that is violation of a fundamental right.

I have dismantled this network now.

10. What can one do?

If you use Linux you can have a Pendrive with your favorite distribution to boot up.

That is the cheapest way.

Otherwise have your own netbook or laptop which is bulky to say the least.

With tablets coming the weight might come down a little.

Apart from other reasons, this is one reason, I strongly support tablets with variety of android clones and in time to come Anti-Android from Singapore.

Story

I wanted to show JoliCloud to a young guy.

I logged in his computer with my password.

Browser Chrome.

Operating system Microsoft Win 7.

I tried to log off the cookie wasn't there.

Tried several times, searched every godforsaken little menu but could not log off.

I log on to JoliCloud, it starts again to my cloud space without asking for the password.

No logging off dialog box.

Finally he had to erase the one hour of our activity to erase the cookies remembering my password for future sessions.

Had I left without logging off he would have had the access to my data and if he devised (he was a nice guy and I was pretty sure he would not do that) a method to change my password I will lose my ability to log in next time.

The story is different if the guy is like your paranoid boss. I signed off saying there is no privacy in the web.

He agreed without reservation.

I hate almost all the web browsers in current use except light weight Linux derivatives.

Linux derivatives are light on your computer and has utilities to block unnecessary cookies and erase the memory at the end of a web session.

All the web browsers have become bulky over the years and have left enough security holes.

I will list few of the Linux browsers, I like most before talking about the game-changer Amazon-Silk.

I hope it will not become bulky in time but have enough security patches since lot of young kids are going to use it on daily basis.

1.IceApe and its Suite

2. Dillo

3. SeaMonkey

4. IceWeasel

5. Midori

6.Abrowser

Mobile Web Kits

7. Opera Mobile (Mini)

8. Android WebKit

9. Safari

10. BlackBerry WebKit

11. Dolfin-Samsung

12. Nokia WebKit

13. Phantom

14. MicroB-Nokia

15. Firefox Gecko in MeeGo

Note Gecko is a Firefox Light derivative that comes from Linux origin, from good old days of Linux and unfortunately IE and Firefox have to do, quite a lot of work to get to Mobile Industry using them as a default.

IE and Firefox are gorilla derivative of Internet.

I believe Linux distributions should all have some alternative Lightweight web browsers included in their distributions.

It is interesting that SwiftLinux which has done a good job of it in its recent version.

Actually the credit should go to AntiX.

These light weight stuff can be used in Mobile and Cloud Computing and now that Amazon has shown the way by splitting the resources we are going to have frantic activity in this arena with mobile to lure.

Amazon's Silk approach is admirable and it is going to be a game-changer.

I think all the web browsers have to go on a diet soon or have at least two versions.

One for mobile and cloud and the other for the desktop.

Chapter 24

Why I should not go for a new 64 bit computer?

I have many 32 bit computers and they have done the donkey work for me and my family, over the past 5 years and none of them is ready for retirement.

Even if I retire them there is nobody to look after them.

But they are on voluntary retirement, simply because the electricity tariff has gone beyond my purse and control.

It has gone up by 50% and I stopped downloading and subscribed to Linux Magazine from the money saved for one month Electricity bill.

I get a free DVD with every issue.

Buying the print version of the Magazine contributes to my carbon foot-print but I save 10 times carbon foot-print if I switched off the computer for good except for checking my email.

The other reason for me not buying a new computer (64 bits) is that now I can buy a few Raspberry Pis, instead of a computer and tinker it for my liking.

They are going to make a camera outfit soon out of the Raspberry Pi/Pie.

I have only one Refurbished Mini 64 bit computer to test Linux 64 bit versions and it looks like in another five years they may not have 32 bit Linux versions except PCLinux and its FullMonty counterpart which works equally well on 64 bit computers.

Then of course Tablets are going to hit the local market, at least the cheap Chinese versions and buying one of them will cut down my carbon foot-print and the electricity bill.

With an E-reader an email I am all set, all that I may want for my twilight years are bundled in a 10 inch Tablet or Slate and I am back to kindergarten work again.

Think twice before one buys a new or old computer.

Their days seem to be numbered and they will be dumped in this small island including, temples where nobody would use them because of the price hike in electricity.

It is going to be a miracle to get one to use a computer then.

I have a new saying now.

In good old days we said, if one has an enemy, one buys or coax him to buy an old car so that he will spend a fortune to get it in running order.

Now one has to pay a fortune to buy a car let alone run it on the road.

The new saying is "if one has an enemy buy him a laptop or an old computer".

He may never find parts or battery to run it/them and they are loaded with all the Microsoft viruses.

Chapter 25

Ubuntu and its derivatives- an update.

It is more than 3 years of critical writing on Linux.

I am going to call it a day soon since the electricity bill is up and I have decided to cut down on my carbon footprint on this planet.

I need to put the ideas in print and digital forms.

That is in the expectation of these blog ideas will vanish into wilderness when new form factors and new ideas hit the market.

That is natural and one has to move on.

Only book I have not done yet is TQM-Quality for the Developers.

Linux is now matured fully and Quality as an inbuilt system should come into effect since tablets will hit the market and poor old 32 bit computers and many 64 bit computers will be relegated to the attic.

The Quality Cycles of 5 years would do the job and when the Linux community gets a complaint from Window's migrant (Linux guys will quietly will find a fix) one should investigate whether it is due to hardware or software or user learning curve (steep or flat) or Quality issue.

If the issue is not of quality the developer should leave the community to address the problem leaving his or her precious time for consolidation of issues related to the platform he/she is involved in developing.

Equally he / she should see the penetration of the distribution among newbies.

If the distribution does not penetrate it is the fault of the marketing system. May be a virus or aesthetic values or damn indifference of the user.

Ubuntu 12-04

First time in my life I am using Ubuntu as a base for introducing it to the resistant users like my daughter.

If they run into problem at home with any issue with Windows, they are now independent to sit in front of a Linux Box and sort them out themselves, while I am away doing things not related to Linux or house work.

Ubuntu's Unity has matured enough to be recommended to a newbie (if old Linux guys are grumbling, let them do it at their own peril and at lib) and canonical should invest its resources on Mobile Market and Cloud Computing.

1. I recommend Pinguy Linux since it has many derivatives including light weight distributions for netbooks.

2. Linux Regal Titan is a very good one for 64 bits.

3. Black Opal (Ubuntu mix) has sorted out many of the windowing and workplace problems.

4. UberStudent 64 bit is heavy (4 GiB) and I am glad to see they have put out a 32 bit one with less packages (2.5 GiB).

It used to have a CD version too.

5. Ultimate Linux light is a good one for games.

6. ArtistX is for Video, Audio and for the artists.

Then, there are Dream Studio, Ubuntu Studio and many more distributions to cater for many tastes.

Ubuntu is still the number one that has penetrated the mind and soul of average users.

For specialist Linux users there over 300 other distributions which is not Ubuntu, to have a go.

Unfortunately Gentoo derivatives except Sabayon is falling behind and TinHat has to do lot of catch up.

Chapter 26

Time for me to take the stock of Linux Activity

It was more than three years that I constantly investigated the Linux World of Freedom.

There were many frustrations when I could not download, Puppy Linux even in the in the University Setup which was less than 100 MiB.

Running the first Puppy Linux was the height of satisfaction.

I still carry that trait and it is still my favorite distribution.

When I first ran it from a USB Stick, it was the glory of discovering the the freedom.

Getting first Linux distribution which was Redhat Linux running in my 4MiB inbuilt graphic card on P2 Machine was never a failed exercise.

Real reason for my enthusiasm In Linux I should bare it now.

I wanted to have a little workshop for School Children in Kandy and it was total disaster not because I was ill prepared.

Microsoft bribed the guys organizing (with alcohol and money) the function and prevented me from having an audience.

I am one who never take anything lying down in this country.

For that matter any where in the globe.

It was a simple innocent exercise.

Never thought it will blossom to this extent.

I investigated and found the guys (who had left school just 17 plus or 18 plus not able to get into the University).

Unfortunately, those guys published their intention in the web and what I did to them is only a tiny history now and no need to say anything more.

I am still thankful to Microsoft for doing that.

Microsoft inadvertently charged my inner brain faculties.

If they did not do that my enthusiasm in Linux would have petered out in no time.

I had finished my research work in the University and I was looking for something new.

This was a great opportunity and I took Linux head on and later having mastered Linux I took, Microsoft in any position they attack me.

Only once they could do that this time from India and I was up to it in hours and traced the guy to India with open challenge.

He never appeared again on my back.

Guy did not know that I had several computers monitoring which Microsoft could not monitor since all the operating system were pirated ones in Sri-Lanka, to my credit.

Thank god for the Policy of Piracy of Sri-Lankans.

They had no hold and I started talking of Copy Right Law in my city.

To my happiness over twenty in the city (everybody except me had pirated copies then, I had Windows 95) were prosecuted for violating Sinhala Songs and Films.

That hit them really hard and some lost their businesses.

Unfortunately, to this day, it is still going on, even in temples and nobody was prosecuted after that incident (since then to my knowledge).

I did venture into Colombo and got a few guys involved in Linux and I used to get my Linux CDs from (DVD not on the market then) Singapore until one, day I went to Singapore and downloaded my first 20 Linux distributions including Linpus Linux from Taiwan.

Nobody in Singapore knew about Linux then, I believe.

I was there for only two weeks and I came home with a Router (Wireless) and made sure I downloaded one distribution a day.

Writing about Linux was also an accident and the University guys (not academics) were on strike and I had all day from 7 to 5 pm in my office to publish in the web.

Fortunately, I was involved with a British Institute which struck a code not violating Copy Right Law and we were getting young (not University undergraduates) ones to write to improve English.

This site was attacked by somebody for political reasons and knowing Sri-Lankan politics well, when I detected the first intrusion, I dissociated with them for a long period of time until recently.

I deleted all my politically sensitive (not Linux) items when they started running again.

Enough of dirty politics in the world wide web and thanks to Linux I was able to register my presence in the web with many free web sites.

Now I am going to severe some of those connections due to rising cost of Electricity.

Nothing Else.

So it is time for me to thank all those who were inspirational to say the least in the Linux community, including Peter Parfitt.

I have no antipathy with Microsoft now but I have a hearty laugh when one is struggling with Windows with a toned down hype.

Because of this reason, not looking at Microsoft Updates my email is never cluttered and I delete them instantaneously, if they do, at the first glance by reflex action.

Now let me thank all the guys who developed little utilities.

To begin with I hate all the web browsers except perhaps Iceweasel.

Simply because some of isos were interrupted / severed in the last few minuets of their download and having to download them from the very beginning, was pain in my neck.

Browsers good at eavesdropping on you but never help you to begin an activity that was terminated by faulty Telecoms connection or server not ready with a file.

1. I love K-torrent and it had done the donkey work.

2. I love www.linuxtracker.og which was hacked several times by the undesirables.

Thank god my electricity bill was manageable, then.

3. Then Distromania site for storing old copies of Linux.

It went defunct for some time and they are not back again.

4. Thank for all the Linux forums who would have a line or two at their web sites to help my searches.

5. Then www.Softpedia.com Linux page 1.

6. Then the www.Distrowatch.com.

7. Not forgetting the Live CD list.

From that site I managed to download Linux in Singapore.

8. Linux Freedom for having a sample of most of the Linux Distributions.

9. Let me say I hate writers who writes, 10 best distributions which distort the facts often with a Virtual Machines.

Linux counter is trying to rectify this anomaly.

10. Then to my amazement only 32 Sri-Lankan guys were using Linux.

Even in South Africa where Ubuntu originated there were very few using Linux.

11. That made me to do some research and one of my dear friend's son in UK (on my invitation) has already completed his masters (Linux penetration).

I provided him with all the useful information.

I have done some local research in the University and its penetration is less than 2% and slightly higher in the Faculty of Dental Science, may be due to my inputs.

So I will take a break and I want the young guys to follow my footsteps.

I will be reading the Linux magazine regularly and they are doing a very good global promotion.

It is well set and my absence won't be felt much.

If I missed anybody that is not an oversight but my gray matter failing in old age.

12. The work horse for me was K3B.

With out which over 1000 CD/DVD sessions (on Nero would have been a disaster) would not have come without a scratch.

I may say with conviction, less than 10 CD/DVDs failed due to faulty manufacture of the CD/DVD.

That is the strength of the Linux utilities.

13. UnetbootIn is my love and I have about 20 USB sticks for demonstration and I now use SD Cards with Androids hitting the market and Raspberry Pi is doing the rounds in UK where I started my computing work, first and not in USA.

Fortunately USA, guys and girls outnumber Sri-Lankan counterparts, visiting my blog site.

And thanks to all of them who visit my site!

Foot Note

Init Processes

In Unix-based computer operating systems, init (short for initialization) is the first process started during booting of the computer system. Init is a daemon process that continues running until the system is shut down. It is the direct or indirect ancestor of all other processes and automatically adopts all orphaned processes. Init is started by the kernel using a hard-coded filename; a kernel panic will occur if the kernel is unable to start it.

Init is typically assigned process identifier 1.

In Unix systems such as System III and System V, the design of init has diverged from the functionality provided by the init in Research Unix and its BSD derivatives. The usage in most Linux distributions employing a traditional init rather than a recent variant such as systemd is somewhat compatible with System V, while some distributions such as Slackware use BSD-style startup scripts, and Gentoo have their own customized versions.

The systemd is the new init system, starting with Fedora and now adopted in many distributions like RedHat, Suse and Centos.

Historically, most of us have been using traditional SysV init scripts normally residing in /etc/rc.d/init.d/. These scripts invoke a daemon binary which will then fork a background process. Even though shell scripts are very flexible, tasks like supervising processes and parallelized execution ordering are difficult to implement. With the introduction of systemd's new-style daemons it is easier to supervise and control them at runtime and it simplifies their implementation.

However, there is big controversy, even among Debian developers which initialization method to adopt.

Gnome

Every part of GNOME 3 has been designed to make it simple and easy to use. The Activities Overview is an easy way to access all your basic tasks. A press of a button is all it takes to view your open windows, launch applications or check if you have new messages. Having everything in one place is convenient and means that you don't have to learn your way around a maze of different technologies.

Chapter 27

Epilogue

There may be lot of missing items in this book.

I did not try to be comprehensive.

Then it becomes a Linux Bible.

I have avoided partitioning and hardware support deliberately.

Little is changed in partitioning skills except the partitioning type. My only warning is be careful when choosing the new partitioning types.

I tried to be bit narrative this time round instead of being analytical and scientific. The analytical approach was necessary when the Linux was in early stage of development and there was a hype in activity.

Now it is on stable ground except where cutting edge changes are made in the hardware sector.

It is mature and robust now.

One has to make a choice depending on one's needs.

I will summarize my subjective / objective selection for my use and the reader has to decide his / her own choices.

If you are using it as a hobby one need at least two computers (I had 10) or perhaps three one being a laptop/netbook.

One can be dedicated for testing.

Now I have gone down to only one computer, there will be less and less input from me in the immediate future even at web / Internet level.

If I do not put them in writing or in digital form my time testing them would be a void. That is the very reason I am publishing this book for an entry level Linux user to browse before he/she start experimenting with Linux. Teething problems and pain is taken care of, for one who is without a proper Guru.

My choices are

1. General Use

Peppermint for Light Weight

Debian for all six desktops

2. Hobby

Puppy Linux

Knoppix

3. Education

Uberstudent

4. Scientific

Poseidon Linux

5. Technical Use

Dynabolic for Music

ArtistiX for Graphics

Debian for Programming

6. Kids and Games

Picaros Diego

7. Games

Steam OS with New 64 bit computer

Rest of the distributions fall in between those mentioned above. Anyone can be used without a problem as long as there is no conflict with hardware compatibility.

If I am allowed only one choice I would go for Debian because it has vast repository.

I prefer light weight distributions since cloud computing is the way things are moving. I have minimal requirements and that is writing and for that also I find Abiword is just as robust as LibreOffice.

Its outstanding feature is its files are light weight and I can upload and download them quickly. There is another reason its format is dedicated to its platform, so others, cannot steal or modify them from my cloud hosting base unless they have Abiword with them.

One thing that nobody can take away from you is the skills that you have mastered, if you master a skill using one utility or software that remains with you for a Life.

Skills I have learned having migrated from Microsoft to Linux is making my life easy and has expanded my horizon.

There is no limit to my exploration.

I feel free and nobody dare exploit my freedom.

That is a wonderful feeling.

Author's Note

I have tried to put everything in a nutshell.

The idea was to keep it under 200 pages.

It is difficult to keep pace with changing world, Linux included. I hope this book will help one to make value added judgments.

It is not called the master stroke but informative choice in a fast moving world.

It is imperative for one who makes the choice, position himself or herself in an almost stationary poise, ideally with a panoramic view, let the world go by, in front of you but enter the niche that suits you the best, at the right time.

For experimenting with Linux such a strategy is essential.

Quite by accident, I entered the niche and it has done wonders for me.

Why don't you try Linux yourself and see?